CONTENTS

1. Morning Motivation Spell   10
2. Gratitude Stone Spell   13
3. Vision Board Ritual Spell   16
4. Affirmation Jar Spell   20
5. Moonlight Reflection Spell   23
6. Seed Planting Ceremony Spell   29
7. Mirror Affirmations Spell   33
8. Gratitude Walk Spell   37
9. Learning Journal Spell   40
10. Candle Meditation Spell   44
11. Visualization Meditation Spell   47
12. Self-Compassion Bath Spell   51
13. Daily Learning Spell   54
14. Affirmation Bracelet Spell   57
15. Progress Pebbles Spell   60
16. Moon Water Growth Spell   63
17. Crystal Grid for Growth Spell   66

18.	Growth Mindset Sigil Spell	69
19.	Affirmation Stones Spell	72
20.	Sunrise Meditation Spell	75
21.	Positive Letter to Self Spell	78
22.	Herbal Sachet Spell for Growth and Clarity	81
23.	Daily Gratitude Ritual Spell	84
24.	Growth Mindset Candle Spell	87
25.	Nature Meditation Spell	91
26.	Self-Care Day Spell	95
27.	Gratitude Jar Spell	99
28.	Affirmation Mirror Spell	102
29.	Visualization Walk Spell	105
30.	Growth Sigil Meditation Spell	108
31.	Learning Circle Spell	111
32.	Positive Self-Talk Ritual Spell	114
33.	Learning Altar Spell	117
34.	Crystal Infused Water Spell	121
35.	Sunlight Meditation Spell	124
36.	Daily Learning Card Spell	127
37.	Gratitude Stone Circle Spell	130
38.	Visualization Candle Spell	134
39.	Heart Chakra Meditation Spell	138
40.	Positive Affirmation Ritual Spell	141
41.	Learning Tree Spell	145

42.	Cleansing Ritual Spell	148
43.	Gratitude Journal Spell	151
44.	Flower Crown Ritual Spell	154
45.	Self-Love Meditation Spell	157
46.	Positive Letter from the Universe Spell	160
47.	Affirmation Art Spell	163
48.	Daily Growth Card Spell	166
49.	Sunrise Affirmations Spell	169
50.	Gratitude Candle Spell	172

THE WELLNESS WITCH

Spells for Positive Thinking and Mental Resilience

By: The Wellness Witch

To all who dare to embrace magic as a tool for transformation,
Open your heart to the endless possibilities within.

May your spells bring clarity, strength, and purpose,
Your intentions lighting the way forward.

Let every ritual remind you of your boundless potential,
Opening doors to the life you envision. Victories, no
matter how small, are steps toward greatness. Each
moment you spend on your craft is a gift to yourself.

Cherish the journey and the lessons it brings, Honor your
growth and the magic within. As you seek the light, may you
find peace in the process. Shadow and light are both part of your
path, embrace them. In every spell, may you discover your inner
strength. Trust in yourself, for you are capable of incredible
things. You are the author of your own enchanted story.

I wish for your journey to be filled with love, joy, and healing.

Let this book be a companion to your self-discovery.
Over time, may it remind you of your infinite worth.
Vision, resilience, and hope will guide your way. Every
intention you set brings you closer to your dreams.

You are loved, cherished, and supported, always. Open your
arms to the magic of life, and may it bring you peace. Under
every moon and every star, may your light shine brightly.

The **Sun** loved
the **Moon** so much

he **died every night**
to **let her breathe**

The Power of Positivity
in Modern Witchcraft

Positivity is not merely a fleeting emotion or a surface-level affirmation; it is a profound force that shapes the very fabric of our reality. In modern witchcraft, positivity becomes a tool of transformation, a spark that ignites the magic within. By aligning our intentions with positive energy, we open ourselves to the boundless possibilities of the universe. This is not about denying the shadows that life may cast but about embracing the light that resides within us, using it to illuminate our path. Each spell, each ritual, becomes a declaration of hope, a manifestation of resilience, and a step toward a life infused with purpose and joy.

Modern witchcraft teaches us that positivity is not passive; it is an active, deliberate practice. It requires us to cultivate mindfulness, to recognize the power of our thoughts, and to channel them into spells that uplift and empower. When we weave positivity into our craft, we are not only transforming our own lives but also sending ripples of light into the world around us. The herbs we choose, the words we speak, the symbols we draw—all are imbued with the energy of our intent, creating a tapestry of magic that reflects our inner strength.

In the practice of modern spellcraft, positivity

becomes a shield and a beacon. It protects us from the weight of negativity, allowing us to stand firm in the face of challenges. At the same time, it guides us toward growth and healing, reminding us that we are capable of overcoming even the most daunting obstacles. By embracing the power of positivity, we honor our own resilience and step into a space where magic and intention converge, creating a life that is both enchanted and empowered.

Understanding Mental Resilience Through Spellcraft

Mental resilience is the quiet strength within us, the unseen thread that weaves together our ability to endure, adapt, and flourish in the face of challenges. Through the lens of spellcraft, this resilience becomes more than a mere concept—it transforms into a tangible energy we can nurture and amplify. By aligning our intentions with the natural rhythms of the universe, we craft spells that act as anchors, grounding us in moments of turmoil and guiding us back to our center. This practice is not about escaping hardship but embracing it with grace, using the tools of our craft to turn adversity into an opportunity for growth.

Spellcraft offers a sacred space where the mind, spirit,

and universe converge, creating a fertile ground for cultivating mental resilience. Each spell, when cast with intention, becomes a declaration of our inner power and a reminder of our capacity to overcome. Whether it's a simple affirmation whispered under the moonlight or a ritual steeped in ancient tradition, the act of spellcasting invites us to pause, reflect, and reaffirm our strength. In these moments, we are reminded that resilience is not a destination but a journey—a continuous dance between surrender and determination.

To truly understand mental resilience through spellcraft, we must first honor the connection between our inner world and the energies that surround us. The herbs we choose, the words we speak, and the symbols we draw all carry vibrations that resonate with our intentions. By mindfully engaging with these elements, we create a symphony of energy that fortifies our spirit and sharpens our focus. Spellcraft, then, becomes a mirror reflecting our potential—a sacred practice that empowers us to rise, time and time again, with unwavering faith in our ability to thrive.

How to Use This Book Effectively

This book is a journey, not a set of rigid instructions. To use it effectively, approach each spell and ritual with an open heart and a curious mind. Allow yourself the freedom to adapt the practices to your unique energy and intentions. Remember, the magic lies not in the words alone but in the emotions and intentions you pour into them. Let this book be your companion, whispering gentle encouragement as you weave positivity and resilience into your daily life.

Begin by reading through the spells and rituals, letting their essence resonate with your spirit. You don't need to master everything at once—take your time to connect with the practices that speak to you most. Trust that your intuition will guide you to the spells that align with your current needs and desires. This book is not a race; it is a sanctuary where you can return as often as you need.

Finally, treat this book as a living, breathing entity —a reflection of your own spiritual growth. As you evolve, so too will your understanding of the spells and their impact on your life. Keep a journal to document your experiences, insights, and any modifications you make to the rituals. Over time, you'll discover that the true magic is not just in the spells but in the empowered, resilient person you become through their practice.

1. MORNING MOTIVATION SPELL

Ingredients:
- A yellow candle
- A lighter or matches
- Your chosen affirmation

Preparation:
1. Find a quiet and comfortable space where you can focus without distractions.
2. Choose an affirmation that resonates with your intention to embrace challenges and learn from experiences. Examples include:
   - "I welcome challenges as opportunities for growth."
   - "Every experience teaches me valuable lessons."
   - "I am capable of overcoming any obstacle."

Spell Instructions:
1. Set Your Intention:
   - Before lighting the candle, take a moment to center yourself. Close your eyes and take a few deep breaths, inhaling positivity and exhaling any negativity.

2. Light the Candle:

- Use the lighter or matches to light the yellow candle. As you do, focus on the flame and visualize it igniting your inner strength and determination.

3. Recite Your Affirmation:
    - Stand or sit comfortably in front of the candle. Recite your chosen affirmation aloud, with conviction and belief. Feel the words resonate within you, filling you with motivation and a positive mindset.
    - Example: "I welcome challenges as opportunities for growth. Each day, I learn and evolve, becoming stronger and more resilient."

4. Visualize Your Day:
    - With the candle still burning, close your eyes and visualize your day ahead. See yourself confidently facing any challenges, learning from each experience, and growing stronger. Imagine yourself filled with energy, enthusiasm, and a sense of purpose.

5. Seal the Spell:
    - After reciting your affirmation and visualizing your day, let the candle burn for a few more minutes as you absorb the energy and intention you've set. When you feel ready, extinguish the candle safely, knowing that the motivation and positive energy will stay with you throughout the day.

6. Daily Practice:
    - Repeat this spell each morning to start your day with motivation and a growth mindset. You can use

the same affirmation or choose a new one each day that aligns with your goals and intentions.

Additional Tips:
- Keep a journal to record your experiences and reflections each day. Note how the spell influences your mindset and actions.
- If you can't light a candle, you can still perform this spell by simply reciting the affirmation and visualizing your day.

By incorporating this Morning Motivation Spell into your daily routine, you'll cultivate a positive mindset that embraces challenges and fosters continuous learning and growth.

2. GRATITUDE STONE SPELL

Ingredients:
- A small, smooth stone
- A marker or paint (optional)
- A quiet space

Preparation:
1. Find a small stone that feels comfortable to hold and carry in your pocket. Ideally, it should be smooth and fit easily in your hand.
2. If desired, you can decorate the stone with a symbol, word, or color that represents gratitude and growth to you.

Spell Instructions:
1. Set Your Intention:
   - Sit in a quiet space where you won't be disturbed. Hold the stone in your hand and close your eyes. Take a few deep breaths, inhaling positivity and exhaling any tension.

2. Imbue the Stone with Energy:
   - Focus on the stone in your hand. Visualize it glowing with a warm, golden light. Imagine this light filling the stone with the energy of gratitude and

growth.

3. State Your Intention:
   - Speak aloud your intention for the stone. You can say something like:
     - "This stone is a symbol of my gratitude and my journey of growth. Every time I touch it, I will remember something I am grateful for that contributes to my personal development."

4. Charge the Stone:
   - Hold the stone close to your heart and take a moment to think of one specific thing you are grateful for that has helped you grow. Feel the gratitude filling your heart and flowing into the stone.
   - Example: "I am grateful for my ability to learn from my mistakes and grow stronger each day."

5. Carry the Stone:
   - Keep the stone in your pocket or a place where you can easily touch it throughout the day. Each time you feel the stone, take a moment to think of one new thing you are grateful for that contributes to your growth.

6. Daily Practice:
   - Make it a habit to touch the stone and think of a new thing you're grateful for every day. This practice will help reinforce a positive mindset and keep you focused on your personal growth.

Additional Tips:
- You can recharge the stone's energy periodically by repeating the steps of this spell, especially if you feel its energy waning.
- Consider keeping a gratitude journal to accompany this spell, where you can write down the things you are grateful for each day.
- If you have more than one stone, you can rotate them to keep the practice fresh and meaningful.

By carrying your Gratitude Stone and regularly reflecting on the things you are thankful for, you will cultivate a positive attitude and a mindset that is conducive to continuous growth and self-improvement.

3. VISION BOARD RITUAL SPELL

Ingredients:
- A large piece of poster board or corkboard
- Magazines, printouts, or images and words that resonate with your goals and dreams
- Scissors
- Glue, tape, or push pins
- Markers or pens
- A quiet and dedicated space
- A candle (optional)

Preparation:
1. Gather all the materials you will need for creating your vision board. Make sure you have a variety of images, words, and quotes that inspire you and represent your goals and dreams.
2. Find a quiet space where you can focus without interruptions. If you wish, you can light a candle to create a sacred and calming atmosphere.

Spell Instructions:
1. Set Your Intention:
   - Before you begin, take a moment to sit quietly and center yourself. Close your eyes and take a few

deep breaths, inhaling positivity and exhaling any distractions or negativity.

- Think about your goals and dreams, and set a clear intention for what you want to manifest in your life. You can say something like:

    - "I create this vision board to manifest my goals and dreams. May these images and words guide me towards my highest potential and deepest desires."

2. Create the Vision Board:

- Begin by selecting images, words, and quotes that resonate with your goals and dreams. Cut them out and arrange them on your board.

- As you place each item on the board, focus on the intention behind it. Visualize yourself achieving that goal or living that dream.

- Glue, tape, or pin each item to the board in a way that feels visually pleasing and inspiring to you.

3. Enhance with Personal Touches:

- Use markers or pens to add your own words, affirmations, or drawings to the board. Personalize it with elements that make it uniquely yours.

- You can also write a powerful affirmation or mantra at the center of the board to serve as a focal point.

4. Activate Your Vision Board:

- Once you have completed your vision board, take a moment to sit quietly in front of it. Light the candle if you are using one, and allow its light to illuminate your board.

- Place your hands over your heart and take a few deep breaths. Visualize your goals and dreams coming to fruition. Feel the emotions associated with achieving them—joy, gratitude, excitement, and fulfillment.
- Say aloud: "I am open to receiving the opportunities and guidance that will lead me to my goals. I trust in the process and believe in my ability to manifest my dreams."

5. Daily Practice:
- Place your vision board in a prominent location where you will see it daily, such as your bedroom, office, or a dedicated altar space.
- Spend a few minutes each day looking at your vision board. Visualize your goals and dreams coming true, and feel the positive emotions associated with them.
- Use the vision board as a source of inspiration and motivation, reminding you of your intentions and keeping you focused on your path.

Additional Tips:
- Update your vision board as needed to reflect new goals, dreams, or changes in your life.
- Consider creating smaller, themed vision boards for specific areas of your life, such as career, relationships, health, or personal development.
- Share your vision board with supportive friends or family members who can help encourage and motivate you.

By creating and using your Vision Board with intention, you harness the power of visualization and positive thinking to manifest your goals and dreams. This ritual serves as a constant reminder of your aspirations and keeps you aligned with your true desires.

4. AFFIRMATION JAR SPELL

Ingredients:
- A glass jar or any container with a lid
- Slips of paper or sticky notes
- Pens or markers
- A quiet and comfortable space

Preparation:
1. Gather your materials and find a quiet space where you can focus and write without interruptions.
2. Think about the positive affirmations that resonate with you and support your personal growth and mindset. Examples include:
   - "I am capable of achieving my goals."
   - "I embrace challenges as opportunities to grow."
   - "I am worthy of love and success."
   - "Every day, I become a better version of myself."

Spell Instructions:
1. Set Your Intention:
   - Sit quietly and take a few deep breaths to center yourself. Close your eyes and focus on your intention to cultivate a growth mindset and embrace positive change.
   - Say aloud: "I create this affirmation jar to inspire and uplift me each day. May these affirmations guide

me towards growth, self-love, and positivity."

2. Write Affirmations:
   - On each slip of paper, write a different positive affirmation. As you write each one, focus on its meaning and how it applies to your life. Visualize the affirmation becoming a reality.
   - Fold the slips of paper and place them in the jar.

3. Charge the Jar:
   - Hold the jar in your hands and close your eyes. Visualize a bright, warm light surrounding the jar, filling it with positive energy and intention.
   - Say aloud: "This jar is filled with affirmations that will guide me, support me, and help me grow each day. I trust in the power of these words to transform my life."

4. Daily Practice:
   - Each morning, take a moment to sit quietly and breathe deeply. Open the jar and pull out one slip of paper.
   - Read the affirmation aloud and reflect on its meaning. Consider how you can incorporate its message into your day and focus on it throughout your activities.
   - Keep the affirmation with you if possible, or place it somewhere you'll see it frequently, like your desk or bathroom mirror.

5. Replenish as Needed:

- Periodically add new affirmations to the jar to keep the practice fresh and relevant to your current goals and experiences.
- You can also share this practice with friends or family members by inviting them to contribute their own affirmations to your jar.

Additional Tips:
- Personalize your jar by decorating it with symbols, colors, or words that inspire you.
- Consider pairing this practice with journaling. Write about your reflections on each day's affirmation and how it influences your thoughts and actions.
- Use this ritual as a moment of self-care and mindfulness, helping you start each day with a positive and intentional mindset.

By incorporating this Affirmation Jar Spell into your daily routine, you'll create a powerful habit of focusing on positive thoughts and nurturing a growth mindset. This simple yet meaningful practice will help you stay motivated, inspired, and aligned with your personal goals.

5. MOONLIGHT REFLECTION SPELL

Moon phases are closely tied to the process of setting and working with intentions. Each phase has distinct energy, which can enhance specific types of goals and actions. Here's a breakdown of the moon phases and how they align with intention-setting:

1. New Moon (Beginnings, Planting Seeds)
Energy: A time of stillness and potential. Represents new beginnings and planting the seeds of your intentions.
Best for: Setting intentions, starting new projects, or reflecting on what you want to manifest in your life.
Ritual Idea: Write down your intentions on paper. Focus on clarity and purpose, as this is the foundational phase for your goals.

2. Waxing Crescent Moon (Building Momentum)
Energy: Growth, motivation, and forward movement. This phase encourages nurturing your intentions.
Best for: Planning, taking initial steps toward your goals, and building confidence.
Ritual Idea: Visualize your intentions daily and take small, actionable steps to bring them to life.

3. First Quarter Moon (Action and Overcoming Challenges)
Energy: A time of action, decision-making, and problem-solving. Challenges may arise, requiring persistence.
Best for: Taking decisive action and tackling obstacles that stand in the way of your intentions.
Ritual Idea: Reflect on any resistance or challenges and reaffirm your commitment to your goals. Adjust plans if necessary.

4. Waxing Gibbous Moon (Refinement and Focus)
Energy: A time to refine and tweak your efforts. The energy builds toward the full moon.
Best for: Reviewing progress, refining intentions, and ensuring alignment with your goals.
Ritual Idea: Meditate on what's working and what isn't. Release distractions and focus on fine-tuning your actions.

5. Full Moon (Manifestation and Celebration)
Energy: A culmination of energy and intentions. Represents clarity, illumination, and results.
Best for: Reaping the rewards of your efforts, celebrating progress, and releasing what no longer serves you.
Ritual Idea: Perform a gratitude practice, express what you've achieved, and release any lingering doubts or negativity through journaling or a cleansing ritual.

6. Waning Gibbous Moon (Gratitude and Sharing)

Energy: A time of gratitude, introspection, and sharing your insights with others.
Best for: Reflecting on lessons learned and preparing to let go of what isn't serving your highest good.
Ritual Idea: Write down what you're grateful for and share your successes or wisdom with others.

7. Last Quarter Moon (Release and Letting Go)
Energy: A phase of release, letting go, and clearing space for new beginnings.
Best for: Ending unhelpful patterns, clearing clutter (mental or physical), and preparing for a fresh start.
Ritual Idea: Perform a releasing ritual, such as writing down what you want to let go of and burning the paper safely to symbolize release.

8. Waning Crescent Moon (Rest and Reflection)
Energy: A time of rest, surrender, and preparation for the new moon cycle. The energy is introspective and restorative.
Best for: Reflecting on the past cycle, meditating, and planning for the future.
Ritual Idea: Engage in deep relaxation or meditation. Reflect on your journey and visualize where you want to focus in the next cycle.

Tips for Setting Intentions with the Moon Phases
1. Be Clear and Specific: Ensure your intentions are well-defined and actionable.
2. Write Them Down: Writing solidifies your goals and creates a tangible connection to your intentions.

3. Work with the Moon's Energy: Align your actions with the moon phase for optimal energetic support.
4. Reflect Regularly: Use each phase as a checkpoint to evaluate progress and adjust your efforts.
5. Practice Gratitude: Regularly give thanks for what you've achieved and the opportunities for growth.

Ingredients:
- A comfortable outdoor space where you can sit under the full moon
- A journal or notebook
- A pen or pencil
- A candle (optional)
- A quiet and peaceful setting

Preparation:
1. Choose a night when the moon is full and the sky is clear. Find a comfortable spot outdoors where you can sit and have a clear view of the moon.
2. Bring your journal, pen, and candle (if using) to your chosen spot.

Spell Instructions:
1. Set Your Space:
   - If you're using a candle, light it to create a sacred space and to help focus your mind. Place the candle safely where it won't be disturbed by the wind.
   - Sit comfortably and take a few deep breaths to center yourself. Close your eyes for a moment and feel the energy of the full moon surrounding you.

2. Reflect on Your Progress:
 - Open your journal and think about the past month. Consider the goals you set, the challenges you faced, and the progress you made. Reflect on both your successes and the lessons learned from any setbacks.
   - Write about your experiences, focusing on how you've grown and what you've achieved. Acknowledge your efforts and celebrate your progress, no matter how small.

3. Set New Intentions:
 - Once you've reflected on the past month, turn your attention to the future. Think about what you want to achieve and how you want to grow in the coming month.
  - Write down your new intentions and goals. Be specific and positive, focusing on what you want to attract and manifest in your life.

4. Moonlight Meditation:
  - Close your journal and place it beside you. Sit comfortably and gaze at the full moon. Feel its light washing over you, filling you with calm and clarity.
 - Visualize your new intentions and goals as if they are already coming to fruition. See yourself taking the steps needed to achieve them and feel the emotions associated with your success.

5. Affirm Your Intentions:
  - Speak your intentions aloud, letting the energy of

your words merge with the moonlight. You can say something like:
- "Under the light of this full moon, I honor my progress and set new intentions for growth. I embrace the journey ahead and trust in my ability to achieve my goals."

6. Close the Spell:
- Take a few more deep breaths, feeling the moon's energy reinforcing your intentions. If you lit a candle, blow it out safely, symbolizing the end of the ritual but the continuation of your journey.
- Thank the moon for its guidance and energy, and slowly bring yourself back to the present moment.

Additional Tips:
- You can perform this spell every full moon to track your progress and continually set new intentions.
- Consider using crystals like moonstone or selenite to enhance the moon's energy during your ritual.
- If weather or circumstances prevent you from being outside, you can perform this ritual indoors by a window where you can see the moon, or visualize the moonlight surrounding you.

By engaging in this Moonlight Reflection Spell, you create a powerful ritual of self-assessment and intention-setting, harnessing the energy of the full moon to support your personal growth and development.

6. SEED PLANTING CEREMONY SPELL

Ingredients:
- A small pot or planter
- Soil or potting mix
- Seeds (choose a plant that resonates with growth, such as sunflowers, herbs, or flowers)
- A small trowel or spoon
- Water
- A quiet and dedicated space

Preparation:
1. Gather all your materials and find a quiet space where you can focus on the ceremony without interruptions.
2. Choose a type of seed that symbolizes growth and resonates with you personally.

Spell Instructions:
1. Set Your Intention:
   - Sit quietly for a moment, holding the seeds in your hands. Close your eyes and take a few deep breaths to center yourself.
   - Focus on your intention for growth and development. Visualize yourself achieving your goals and growing in the areas of your life that you want to

nurture.

2. Prepare the Soil:
   - Place the soil or potting mix in the pot, filling it almost to the top. As you handle the soil, think about the foundation you are creating for your growth.

3. Plant the Seed:
   - Make a small hole in the soil with your finger or a small trowel. Place the seed in the hole and cover it lightly with soil.
   - As you plant the seed, say aloud:
     - "As I plant this seed, I plant the seeds of my own growth and development. May it grow strong and healthy, just as I will grow and flourish."

4. Water the Seed:
   - Gently water the seed, providing it with the nourishment it needs to begin its growth journey. As you water the seed, visualize yourself receiving the nourishment and support you need to grow.
   - Say aloud:
     - "With this water, I nourish my growth. May my intentions be nurtured and may I flourish in all aspects of my life."

5. Place the Pot:
   - Place the pot in a location where it will receive adequate light and care. Make sure it is in a spot where you will see it regularly, reminding you of your intention for growth.

6. Daily Care and Visualization:
   - Each day, take a moment to care for the plant. As you water it and check on its progress, visualize your own growth and development.
   - Speak words of encouragement to both the plant and yourself, affirming your intentions and dedication to personal growth.

7. Celebrate Growth:
   - As the seed begins to sprout and grow, celebrate each milestone. Reflect on your own progress and acknowledge the steps you have taken towards your goals.

Additional Tips:
- Keep a journal to document both the growth of your plant and your own personal growth. Note any changes, challenges, and successes you experience.
- Use this ceremony as a recurring ritual, planting new seeds for different goals and intentions as you achieve previous ones.
- Consider incorporating other elements like crystals or small tokens into the soil to further enhance the energy of your intentions.

By performing this Seed Planting Ceremony Spell, you create a tangible connection between your intentions and the natural growth process. This ritual serves as a powerful reminder of your commitment to personal development and the nurturing of your dreams.

SPELLS FOR POSITIVE THINKING AND MENTAL RESILIENCE

7. MIRROR AFFIRMATIONS SPELL

Ingredients:
- A mirror (preferably handheld or a mirror where you can see your entire face)
- A quiet and private space
- A list of affirmations focused on growth and learning

Preparation:
1. Find a quiet space where you can be alone and undisturbed. Have your mirror and list of affirmations ready.
2. Take a few moments to center yourself with deep, calming breaths. Focus on your intention to embrace growth and learning.

Spell Instructions:
1. Set Your Intention:
   - Hold the mirror in your hands or place it where you can clearly see your reflection.
   - Close your eyes and take a few deep breaths, grounding yourself in the present moment. Visualize a bright, warm light surrounding you, filling you with confidence and positivity.

2. Speak Your Affirmations:
- Open your eyes and look directly into your reflection. Gaze into your own eyes, connecting with your inner self.
- One by one, recite your affirmations aloud. Speak each affirmation slowly and clearly, allowing the words to resonate deeply within you. Examples of affirmations you might use include:
  - "I am capable of learning and growing every day."
  - "I embrace challenges as opportunities for growth."
  - "I believe in my ability to achieve my goals."
  - "I am constantly evolving and improving."
  - "I am proud of my progress and excited for my future."

3. Feel the Affirmations:
- As you speak each affirmation, feel the truth of the words sinking into your being. Visualize the positive energy of the affirmations filling your mind and body, strengthening your resolve and confidence.

4. Repeat and Reinforce:
- Repeat each affirmation three times, each time with more conviction and belief. Allow the power of the affirmations to build within you, reinforcing your commitment to growth and learning.

5. Close the Spell:
- After you have spoken all your affirmations, take a moment to thank yourself for taking this step towards self-improvement. Smile at your reflection,

acknowledging your efforts and dedication.
   - Close your eyes and take a few deep breaths, imagining the positive energy of the affirmations continuing to flow within you, even after the spell is complete.

6. Daily Practice:
   - Incorporate this mirror affirmation ritual into your daily routine, ideally in the morning to set a positive tone for the day.
   - Keep your list of affirmations nearby and add new ones as you discover more aspects of yourself that you wish to nurture and grow.

 Additional Tips:
- Customize your affirmations to address specific areas of growth and learning that are important to you.
- Consider using a small mirror that you can carry with you, allowing you to perform this ritual wherever you are, especially when you need a boost of confidence.
- Complement this ritual with journaling, writing down your thoughts and experiences related to the affirmations and the growth you observe in yourself.

By engaging in this Mirror Affirmations Spell, you harness the power of positive self-talk and visualization to cultivate a mindset of continuous growth and learning. This ritual not only boosts your confidence but also reinforces your commitment to personal development.

8. GRATITUDE WALK SPELL

Ingredients:
- Comfortable walking shoes
- A journal or notebook (optional)
- A pen or pencil (optional)
- A quiet, natural setting (park, forest, beach, etc.)

Preparation:
1. Choose a peaceful natural location where you can walk without distractions.
2. Wear comfortable clothing and shoes suitable for walking.
3. Bring your journal and pen if you wish to document your thoughts and experiences.

Spell Instructions:
1. Set Your Intention:
  - Before you begin your walk, stand quietly and close your eyes. Take a few deep breaths to center yourself.
  - Set the intention to focus on gratitude and your ability to grow. Visualize a warm light surrounding you, filling you with a sense of peace and appreciation.

2. Begin Your Walk:
  - Start walking at a slow, steady pace. As you walk,

take in the beauty of your surroundings. Notice the colors, sounds, smells, and textures of nature.
   - With each step, consciously bring your attention to something you are grateful for. This could be something specific in your life, an aspect of yourself, or simply the beauty of the nature around you.

3. Express Gratitude:
   - As you notice things you are grateful for, say a silent or spoken "thank you" for each one. For example:
   - "Thank you for the fresh air I'm breathing."
   - "Thank you for the strength in my body that allows me to walk."
   - "Thank you for the beauty of these flowers."
   - "Thank you for my ability to learn and grow every day."

4. Reflect on Growth:
   - After you've walked for a while, find a comfortable spot to sit and reflect. Close your eyes and think about the personal growth you've experienced recently.
   - Consider the challenges you've overcome, the skills you've developed, and the ways you've evolved. Feel gratitude for your resilience and your journey.

5. Optional Journaling:
   - If you brought your journal, take a few minutes to write down your reflections. Document what you're grateful for and how you've grown. This can help reinforce your positive thoughts and serve as a reminder of your progress.

- Write down any insights or feelings that arose during your walk, focusing on gratitude and growth.

6. Conclude Your Walk:
- When you're ready, continue your walk back. As you walk, keep the feeling of gratitude and growth in your heart.
- Finish your walk with a final moment of thanks. Stand still, take a deep breath, and say, "I am grateful for my growth and the journey I am on."

Additional Tips:
- Make this gratitude walk a regular practice, such as weekly or monthly, to continually reconnect with your sense of gratitude and track your personal growth.
- If you encounter a particular natural element (like a tree, rock, or stream) that resonates with you, spend a few moments there, expressing your gratitude and drawing inspiration from it.
- Share this practice with a friend or loved one to enhance the experience and share mutual gratitude.

By performing this Gratitude Walk Spell, you create a mindful practice that combines physical activity with a focus on gratitude and personal growth. This ritual helps you appreciate the present moment, recognize your progress, and cultivate a positive mindset for continued development.

9. LEARNING JOURNAL SPELL

Ingredients:
- A journal or notebook
- A pen or pencil
- A quiet and comfortable space

Preparation:
1. Choose a journal that resonates with you, something that feels special and inviting.
2. Find a pen or pencil that you enjoy writing with.
3. Set aside a specific time each day for this ritual, preferably in the evening to reflect on the day's experiences.

Spell Instructions:
1. Set Your Intention:
   - Sit in your quiet space with your journal and pen. Take a few deep breaths to center yourself.
   - Close your eyes and set the intention to focus on learning and growth. Visualize a bright light surrounding you, filling you with curiosity and a desire for knowledge.

2. Open Your Journal:
   - Open your journal to a fresh page. At the top, write

the date to mark the day's entry.
- Create a title for your entry that reflects the theme of learning and growth. For example, "Daily Lessons" or "Today's Insights."

3. Reflect on Your Day:
- Take a few moments to think about your day. Consider everything you did, the interactions you had, and any new information or experiences you encountered.
- Ask yourself the following questions:
  - What did I learn today?
  - How did I apply what I learned?
  - What challenges did I face, and how did I overcome them?
  - What insights or realizations did I have?

4. Write Your Entry:
- Begin writing your reflections in the journal. Be honest and detailed, capturing the essence of what you learned and how you applied it.
- For example:
    - "Today, I learned about effective time management techniques. I applied this by creating a more structured schedule for my tasks, which helped me be more productive."
- "I faced a challenge with a difficult project at work. By asking for help and collaborating with my team, I was able to find a solution."

5. Affirm Your Growth:

- After writing your reflections, write a positive affirmation at the end of your entry. This affirmation should focus on your commitment to continuous learning and growth.
- For example:
  - "I am always open to learning new things and applying them in my life."
  - "Each day, I grow stronger and more knowledgeable."

6. Close Your Journal:
- Close your journal with a sense of accomplishment and gratitude. Thank yourself for taking the time to reflect on your learning and growth.
- Take a few deep breaths, imagining the knowledge you've gained settling into your mind and body, strengthening your resolve to keep learning.

7. Repeat Daily:
- Make this journaling ritual a daily practice. Over time, you'll have a valuable record of your learning journey and personal growth.

Additional Tips:
- Review past entries periodically to see how much you've grown and to reinforce the lessons you've learned.
- Customize your journal with drawings, stickers, or other decorations that inspire you and make the practice enjoyable.
- Share insights from your journal with a friend

or mentor to gain additional perspectives and encouragement.

By keeping a Learning Journal, you create a dedicated space for reflecting on your daily experiences and the knowledge you acquire. This ritual not only enhances your learning process but also fosters a growth mindset and a deeper appreciation for your personal development.

10. CANDLE MEDITATION SPELL

Ingredients:
- A green candle
- Matches or a lighter
- A quiet and comfortable space

Preparation:
1. Choose a green candle that resonates with you. Green symbolizes growth, abundance, and renewal, making it perfect for this meditation.
2. Find a quiet space where you can sit comfortably without distractions.

Spell Instructions:
1. Set Your Intention:
   - Sit in a comfortable position with your back straight and your feet flat on the floor. Hold the green candle in your hands.
   - Close your eyes and take a few deep breaths to center yourself. Set the intention for this meditation to focus on your personal growth and potential.

2. Light the Candle:
   - When you feel ready, use matches or a lighter to carefully light the green candle. As you do so,

visualize the flame as a symbol of your inner light and potential.

3. Meditation:
- Once the candle is lit, place it in front of you at eye level. Gaze at the flame and allow your mind to relax.
- As you continue to focus on the flame, let your thoughts drift away. If your mind wanders, gently bring your focus back to the candle.
- With each breath, imagine yourself surrounded by a green light, symbolizing growth and abundance.
- Reflect on your personal growth journey. Consider the progress you've made, the challenges you've overcome, and the potential that lies within you.
- Visualize yourself stepping into your highest potential, embodying the person you aspire to be.
- Allow yourself to feel a sense of empowerment and confidence in your ability to grow and evolve.

4. Duration:
- Meditate on the flame for at least 10 minutes, or longer if you feel called to do so. Allow yourself to fully immerse in the experience.

5. Closing the Meditation:
- When you're ready to end the meditation, gently open your eyes and extinguish the candle flame.
- Take a moment to thank yourself for dedicating this time to your personal growth and potential.
- Carry the energy of the meditation with you throughout your day, knowing that you are supported

in your journey of growth and evolution.

Additional Tips:
- You can enhance this meditation by incorporating soothing music or nature sounds in the background.
- Experiment with different times of day for your candle meditation to see what works best for you.
- Keep a journal nearby to jot down any insights or inspirations that arise during the meditation.

By practicing this Candle Meditation Spell regularly, you create a sacred space for honoring your personal growth and potential. The green candle serves as a powerful symbol of your inner light and the limitless possibilities that await you on your journey of self-discovery and evolution.

11. VISUALIZATION MEDITATION SPELL

Ingredients:
- A quiet and comfortable space
- A comfortable seat or cushion
- Relaxing background music or nature sounds (optional)

Preparation:
1. Find a quiet space where you can sit comfortably without distractions.
2. Settle into a comfortable seat or cushion, ensuring that your back is straight and your body is relaxed.
3. If desired, play relaxing background music or nature sounds to enhance the atmosphere.

Spell Instructions:
1. Set Your Intention:
   - Close your eyes and take a few deep breaths to center yourself. Set the intention for this meditation to focus on visualization and manifestation.
   - Visualize a bright, warm light surrounding you, filling you with a sense of peace and empowerment.

2. Relax Your Body:
   - Start by relaxing your body from head to toe. Take

a few moments to release any tension or tightness you may be holding onto.
- Relax your facial muscles, soften your shoulders, and let your arms and hands rest comfortably in your lap.

3. Visualize Your Goals:
- With your eyes closed, begin to visualize your goals as if they have already been achieved. Picture yourself living your dream life, accomplishing your aspirations, and experiencing your desired outcomes.
- Engage all your senses in the visualization. Imagine what you would see, hear, feel, smell, and taste in your ideal reality.
- Allow yourself to fully immerse in the visualization, feeling the emotions of joy, fulfillment, and gratitude as if your goals have already manifested.

4. Overcome Challenges:
- As you visualize your goals, acknowledge any challenges or obstacles that may arise along the way. See yourself overcoming these challenges with resilience, determination, and grace.
- Visualize yourself finding creative solutions, seeking support when needed, and staying focused on your path despite any setbacks.

5. Anchor the Visualization:
- Once you have fully visualized your goals and overcome challenges, take a moment to anchor the

visualization in your mind.
   - Repeat a positive affirmation or mantra related to your goals. For example:
     - "I am capable of achieving my dreams."
     - "I am worthy of success and abundance."
     - "I trust in the journey and embrace the challenges along the way."

6. Gratitude and Release:
   - Express gratitude for the visualization experience and for the manifestation of your goals. Thank yourself for taking the time to nurture your dreams and aspirations.
   - Release any attachment to the outcome of the visualization. Trust that the universe is working in your favor and that your goals will manifest in divine timing.

7. Return to the Present:
   - When you're ready, slowly bring your awareness back to the present moment. Wiggle your fingers and toes, gently stretch your body, and open your eyes.
   - Take a few moments to reflect on the visualization experience and how it made you feel. Carry this sense of empowerment and possibility with you as you continue your day.

 Additional Tips:
- Practice this Visualization Meditation Spell regularly to reinforce your goals and intentions.
- Keep a journal nearby to write down any

insights, inspirations, or visions that arise during the meditation.
- Experiment with different visualizations, focusing on various aspects of your life and goals.

By engaging in this Visualization Meditation Spell, you harness the power of your imagination to manifest your dreams and aspirations. This ritual helps you align your thoughts, emotions, and actions with your desired outcomes, paving the way for their manifestation in your reality.

12. SELF-COMPASSION BATH SPELL

Ingredients:
- Dried lavender flowers
- Dried chamomile flowers
- A bathtub filled with warm water
- Optional: Relaxing music or candles for ambiance

Preparation:
1. Fill your bathtub with warm water to your desired level.
2. Sprinkle a handful of dried lavender flowers and a handful of dried chamomile flowers into the water.
3. Optional: Set the mood by lighting candles around the bathtub or playing relaxing music in the background.

Spell Instructions:
1. Set Your Intention:
   - Stand beside the bathtub and take a few deep breaths to center yourself.
   - Close your eyes and set the intention for this bath to be a nurturing experience of self-compassion and kindness towards yourself.

2. Step Into the Bath:

- Slowly ease yourself into the warm water, allowing your body to relax and unwind.
- Feel the soothing warmth enveloping you, easing away tension and stress.

3. Affirm Your Self-Compassion:
- With your eyes closed, take a moment to affirm your ability to learn from mistakes with kindness and self-compassion.
- Repeat affirmations such as:
- "I am worthy of kindness, especially from myself."
- "I embrace my mistakes as opportunities for growth and learning."
- "I forgive myself for any perceived shortcomings and treat myself with compassion."

4. Visualize Healing Light:
- Visualize a gentle, healing light surrounding you, bathing you in its warmth and love.
- Imagine this light penetrating deep into your being, soothing any areas of tension or self-judgment.

5. Soak and Reflect:
- Allow yourself to soak in the bath for as long as you like, focusing on the affirmations and visualizations.
- Reflect on moments when you have shown yourself kindness and compassion, and affirm your commitment to continue doing so.

6. Express Gratitude:
- As you soak in the bath, express gratitude for your

body, mind, and spirit. Appreciate yourself for taking this time for self-care and self-compassion.

7. Closing the Ritual:
  - When you feel ready to conclude the ritual, slowly rise from the bath and step out onto a soft towel.
   - Take a moment to inhale deeply and exhale any remaining tension or stress.
   - Carry the sense of self-compassion and kindness with you as you continue your day.

 Additional Tips:
- Enhance the experience by incorporating soothing music or guided meditation while you soak in the bath.
- Practice this Self-Compassion Bath Spell regularly, especially during times when you need to nurture yourself and cultivate self-compassion.
- Consider journaling about your experience after the bath to reflect on any insights or feelings that arose during the ritual.

By engaging in this Self-Compassion Bath Spell, you create a sacred space for nurturing yourself with kindness and compassion. This ritual helps you cultivate a deeper sense of self-love and acceptance, allowing you to embrace your mistakes and imperfections with grace and understanding.

13. DAILY LEARNING SPELL

Ingredients:
- A quiet and focused mind
- Willingness to embrace new experiences
- A journal or notebook (optional)

Preparation:
1. Find a quiet and comfortable space where you can focus without distractions.
2. Set aside a few minutes each day for this ritual, preferably in the morning to set the tone for the day ahead.

Spell Instructions:
1. Set Your Intention:
   - Sit comfortably with your back straight and your feet flat on the floor.
   - Close your eyes and take a few deep breaths to center yourself.
   - Set the intention for the day to be open to learning something new and to embrace new experiences with curiosity and enthusiasm.

2. Affirm Your Intention:
   - Repeat a positive affirmation or mantra related to

learning and growth. For example:
- "I am open to new experiences and opportunities for learning."
- "Each day is an opportunity for growth and expansion."
- "I embrace the unknown with curiosity and excitement."

3. Visualize Your Day:
- Visualize yourself moving through your day with a sense of openness and receptivity to new knowledge and experiences.
- Imagine yourself encountering opportunities for learning in various aspects of your life, whether it's through conversations, observations, or experiences.

4. Be Mindful and Curious:
- Throughout your day, practice mindfulness and curiosity. Pay attention to the world around you and remain open to the lessons it has to offer.
- Approach each experience with a beginner's mind, free from preconceptions or judgments.

5. Reflect on Your Learnings:
- At the end of the day, take a few moments to reflect on what you've learned and experienced.
- Consider jotting down your reflections in a journal or notebook, noting any insights, lessons, or observations that stood out to you.

6. Express Gratitude:

- Express gratitude for the opportunities you had to learn and grow throughout the day.
- Thank yourself for being open to new experiences and for embracing the journey of lifelong learning.

7. Set Tomorrow's Intention:
- Before you go to bed, set an intention for the next day to continue your journey of learning and growth.
- Visualize yourself approaching the day with the same openness and curiosity, ready to discover new insights and expand your understanding of the world.

Additional Tips:
- Keep a learning journal to document your daily learnings and reflections. Reviewing past entries can be a source of inspiration and motivation.
- Share your learnings with others, whether through conversations, blog posts, or social media. Teaching others can deepen your own understanding of the topic.
- Stay open to learning from unexpected sources, including nature, art, and everyday experiences.

By practicing this Daily Learning Spell, you cultivate a mindset of curiosity, growth, and lifelong learning. Each day becomes an opportunity to expand your knowledge, deepen your understanding, and enrich your life with new experiences and insights.

14. AFFIRMATION BRACELET SPELL

Ingredients:
- Beads of your choice (preferably in colors that resonate with growth and positivity)
- Elastic cord or string
- A quiet and focused space
- Positive affirmations for each bead

Preparation:
1. Gather your beads and lay them out in front of you, along with the elastic cord or string.
2. Set aside a few moments to center yourself and clear your mind.

Spell Instructions:
1. Set Your Intention:
   - Sit comfortably with your beads in front of you.
   - Close your eyes and take a few deep breaths to center yourself.
   - Set the intention for this bracelet-making ritual to infuse each bead with a growth-oriented affirmation.

2. Choose Your Affirmations:
   - Take a moment to reflect on areas of your life where you want to cultivate growth and positivity.

- Select affirmations that resonate with your intentions for each bead of the bracelet. These affirmations should focus on personal growth, empowerment, and resilience.

3. String the Beads:
   - Begin stringing the beads onto the elastic cord or string, one by one.
   - As you add each bead, state the corresponding affirmation out loud or silently in your mind. Visualize the affirmation becoming infused into the bead, radiating its positive energy.

4. Empower Your Bracelet:
   - Once all the beads are strung, hold the bracelet in your hands.
   - Close your eyes and visualize the bracelet glowing with vibrant energy, filled with the power of your affirmations.
   - Repeat a final affirmation to seal the energy of the bracelet. For example:
      - "With each bead, I embrace growth and empowerment. This bracelet is a symbol of my inner strength and resilience."

5. Wear Your Bracelet:
   - Slide the bracelet onto your wrist and adjust it to a comfortable fit.
   - Throughout the day, whenever you glance at your bracelet or feel its presence on your wrist, remember the affirmations you've infused into it.

Additional Tips:
- Customize your bracelet with beads in colors that correspond to specific intentions or chakras. For example, green for growth and healing, yellow for confidence and clarity, or purple for intuition and spirituality.
- Revisit your bracelet regularly to reinforce the affirmations and recharge its energy. You can do this by holding it in your hands and repeating the affirmations, or by placing it under sunlight or moonlight for cleansing and renewal.

By crafting this Affirmation Bracelet with intention and mindfulness, you create a wearable talisman that serves as a constant reminder of your commitment to growth and empowerment. Each bead carries the energy of positive affirmations, infusing your daily life with inspiration, resilience, and the potential for transformation.

15. PROGRESS PEBBLES SPELL

Ingredients:
- Small pebbles or stones (collected from nature or purchased)
- A glass jar or container
- A quiet and focused space

Preparation:
1. Collect a handful of small pebbles or stones from a natural outdoor area. Alternatively, you can purchase decorative stones from a craft store.
2. Choose a glass jar or container to serve as your "progress jar."

Spell Instructions:
1. Set Your Intention:
   - Find a quiet and comfortable space where you can focus without distractions.
   - Sit with your pebbles and jar in front of you.
   - Take a few deep breaths to center yourself and set your intention for this ritual. Focus on the idea of progress and growth.

2. Infuse Your Pebbles with Intention:
   - Hold each pebble in your hand and visualize it as a

symbol of your progress and growth.
- State an affirmation or intention for each pebble, such as:
   - "With each step forward, I am growing stronger and more resilient."
   - "Each pebble represents a milestone achieved and a step closer to my goals."

3. Add the Pebbles to the Jar:
- One by one, gently place each pebble into the glass jar or container.
- As you add each pebble, visualize it representing a specific achievement or moment of progress in your life journey.

4. Reflect on Your Progress:
- Take a moment to reflect on the progress you've made so far. Consider the milestones you've reached, the challenges you've overcome, and the growth you've experienced.
- Express gratitude for your progress and acknowledge yourself for your efforts and dedication.

5. Place Your Jar in a Sacred Space:
- Find a special place in your home where you can display your progress jar. It could be on a shelf, a desk, or any area where you'll see it regularly.
- As you place the jar, set the intention for it to serve as a visual reminder of your ongoing growth and achievements.

Additional Tips:
- Consider decorating your progress jar with ribbons, labels, or symbols that represent growth and achievement.
- Regularly update your progress jar by adding new pebbles whenever you achieve a milestone or make significant progress towards your goals.
- Take time to review your progress jar periodically. Reflect on the pebbles you've added and celebrate how far you've come on your journey.

By creating and tending to your Progress Pebbles jar with intention and mindfulness, you cultivate a deeper awareness of your progress and growth over time. Each pebble serves as a tangible reminder of your achievements and milestones, inspiring you to continue moving forward on your path of personal and spiritual development.

16. MOON WATER GROWTH SPELL

Ingredients:
- A clear glass bottle or jar filled with clean water
- Access to a place where you can leave the bottle under the full moonlight
- A quiet and focused space

Preparation:
1. Fill a clear glass bottle or jar with clean water, leaving some space at the top.
2. Set aside a place where you can leave the bottle exposed to the light of the full moon overnight.

Spell Instructions:
1. Set Your Intention:
   - Find a quiet and comfortable space where you can focus without distractions.
   - Hold the bottle of water in your hands and close your eyes.
   - Set your intention for this Moon Water spell to nurture and strengthen your growth mindset.

2. Charge the Water:
   - On the night of the full moon, place the bottle of water in a spot where it will be fully exposed to the

moonlight.
- Leave the bottle there overnight, allowing it to absorb the energy and vibrations of the full moon.

3. Infuse Your Intention:
- The next morning, retrieve the bottle of water from its place under the full moon.
- Hold the bottle in your hands once again and visualize the water glowing with the energy of the moonlight.
- Focus on your intention for nurturing your growth mindset as you hold the bottle.

4. Drink with Intention:
- When you're ready, open the bottle and take a sip of the moon-charged water.
- As you drink, visualize the water flowing into your body, filling you with the energy of growth, expansion, and limitless possibilities.
- Hold the intention of embracing challenges, learning from experiences, and cultivating a mindset of growth and resilience.

5. Express Gratitude:
- After drinking the water, take a moment to express gratitude for the energy of the full moon and for the opportunity to nurture your growth mindset.
- Thank the universe for its support and guidance on your journey of personal and spiritual development.

Additional Tips:

- You can perform this Moon Water Growth Spell during any full moon phase to harness the energy of lunar cycles for nurturing your growth mindset.
- Consider keeping a journal to document your experiences and reflections after drinking the moon-charged water. Notice any shifts in your mindset or awareness over time.
- Use the remaining moon water for other purposes, such as watering plants, cleansing crystals, or blessing sacred objects.

By engaging in this Moon Water Growth Spell, you align yourself with the natural rhythms of the cosmos and harness the potent energy of the full moon to nurture your growth mindset. Each sip of moon-charged water serves as a reminder of your commitment to continuous learning, expansion, and personal evolution.

17. CRYSTAL GRID FOR GROWTH SPELL

Ingredients:
- Green aventurine crystals
- Citrine crystals
- Clear quartz crystals
- A quiet and focused space

Preparation:
1. Gather your green aventurine, citrine, and clear quartz crystals.
2. Find a flat surface where you can arrange the crystals in a grid pattern.
3. Set aside a few minutes to center yourself and clear your mind before beginning the spell.

Spell Instructions:
1. Set Your Intention:
   - Sit comfortably in front of your chosen space and take a few deep breaths to center yourself.
   - Close your eyes and set your intention for the crystal grid to support your growth and expansion in all areas of your life.

2. Arrange the Crystals:
   - Begin by placing the green aventurine crystals in

the center of your grid. This crystal is associated with growth, prosperity, and abundance.
- Surround the green aventurine with citrine crystals, which are known for their energies of manifestation, success, and confidence.
- Finally, place clear quartz crystals around the perimeter of the grid to amplify the energies of the other crystals and enhance their effects.

3. Activate the Grid:
- With all the crystals arranged in the grid, take a moment to connect with their energies.
- Visualize a radiant light flowing from each crystal, forming a cohesive grid of energy that surrounds and supports you.
- Speak your intention aloud or silently in your mind, affirming your desire for growth, expansion, and abundance.

4. Meditate Within the Grid:
- Once the grid is activated, sit or lie down within its center.
- Close your eyes and enter a meditative state, focusing your awareness on the energy of the crystals surrounding you.
- Visualize yourself growing and expanding in all areas of your life, overcoming obstacles, and stepping into your fullest potential.

5. Express Gratitude:
- After your meditation, take a moment to express

gratitude for the support of the crystal grid and for the growth opportunities that lie ahead.
- Thank the crystals for their assistance and the universe for its guidance on your journey.

Additional Tips:
- You can leave the crystal grid set up for as long as you feel it's necessary to support your growth journey. Some people prefer to leave it in place for a few days or even weeks, while others may dismantle it after their meditation session.
- Use your intuition when choosing the size and arrangement of your crystal grid. You may be drawn to certain shapes or patterns that resonate with you and enhance the energy of the grid.
- Regularly cleanse and recharge your crystals to maintain their optimal energy flow and effectiveness in supporting your growth intentions.

By engaging in this Crystal Grid for Growth Spell, you harness the powerful energies of green aventurine, citrine, and clear quartz to support your journey of personal and spiritual development. Through meditation within the grid, you align yourself with the energies of growth, abundance, and expansion, paving the way for transformative experiences and opportunities.

18. GROWTH MINDSET SIGIL SPELL

Ingredients:
- Pen and paper or drawing materials
- A quiet and focused space
- Your intention for cultivating a growth mindset

Preparation:
1. Find a quiet and comfortable space where you can focus without distractions.
2. Set aside a few minutes to clear your mind and center yourself.

Spell Instructions:
1. Set Your Intention:
   - Sit comfortably with your pen and paper in front of you.
   - Take a few deep breaths to center yourself and focus your attention on your intention for cultivating a growth mindset.

2. Create Your Sigil:
   - Visualize the qualities and attributes you associate with a growth mindset, such as resilience, curiosity, and openness to learning.
   - Begin drawing symbols, shapes, and lines that

represent these qualities. Let your intuition guide you as you create your sigil, allowing it to flow naturally from your mind to the paper.

- Don't worry about making it perfect or aesthetically pleasing—focus on capturing the essence of your intention in symbolic form.

3. Charge Your Sigil:
   - Once your sigil is complete, hold it in your hands and focus your attention on it.
   - Close your eyes and visualize your intention for cultivating a growth mindset. Imagine yourself embodying the qualities represented by the sigil—resilient, curious, and open to learning.
   - Channel your energy into the sigil, infusing it with your intention and charging it with the power of your focused intention.

4. Keep It in a Special Place:
   - Find a special place where you can keep your growth mindset sigil.
   - It could be on your desk, altar, or any other space where you'll see it regularly and be reminded of your intention.
   - Treat your sigil with reverence and respect, recognizing it as a potent symbol of your commitment to cultivating a growth mindset.

Additional Tips:
- You can enhance the potency of your growth mindset sigil by incorporating colors, symbols, or

words that resonate with you and reinforce your intention.
- Meditate with your sigil regularly to strengthen your connection to its energy and amplify its effects on your mindset.
- Consider creating multiple copies of your sigil to place in different areas of your home or workspace, spreading its influence throughout your environment.

By creating and charging your Growth Mindset Sigil with intention and focused energy, you create a powerful tool for cultivating a mindset of growth, resilience, and openness to learning. Each time you see your sigil, let it serve as a reminder of your commitment to embracing challenges, seeking opportunities for growth, and realizing your fullest potential.

19. AFFIRMATION STONES SPELL

Ingredients:
- Small stones or pebbles
- Permanent marker or paint pens
- A quiet and focused space

Preparation:
1. Gather small stones or pebbles from your garden, a park, or purchase them from a craft store.
2. Set aside a few minutes to clear your mind and focus your intention on cultivating a growth mindset.

Spell Instructions:
1. Set Your Intention:
   - Sit comfortably with your stones in front of you.
   - Close your eyes and take a few deep breaths to center yourself.
   - Set your intention for this spell to imbue each stone with the energy of growth, resilience, and positivity.

2. Write Your Affirmations:
   - Pick up one stone at a time and hold it in your hand.
   - Reflect on affirmations that resonate with your desire for growth and personal development.
   - Using a permanent marker or paint pen, write

one affirmation on each stone. Examples include "I embrace challenges as opportunities for growth," "I am constantly evolving and improving," and "I believe in my ability to learn and adapt."

3. Place the Stones Around Your Home:
   - Once you've written affirmations on all your stones, place them strategically around your home.
   - You can place them on windowsills, desks, shelves, or any other areas where you'll see them regularly.
   - Arrange the stones in places where they'll catch your eye and serve as constant reminders of your commitment to growth and positivity.

4. Charge the Stones with Intention:
   - Once the stones are in place, take a moment to infuse them with your intention.
   - Close your eyes and visualize each stone glowing with radiant energy, radiating the power of your affirmations into the space around them.
   - Repeat your affirmations aloud or silently in your mind, reinforcing their energy and impact.

Additional Tips:
- You can personalize your affirmations to align with specific areas of growth or challenges you're facing in your life.
- Consider carrying a few affirmation stones with you in a small pouch or pocket for an extra boost of positivity and motivation throughout the day.
- Regularly cleanse and recharge your affirmation

stones to maintain their energy and effectiveness. You can do this by rinsing them under running water or placing them in sunlight or moonlight for a few hours.

By creating and placing Affirmation Stones around your home with intention and purpose, you infuse your living space with the energy of growth, positivity, and resilience. Each time you see or hold a stone, let it serve as a powerful reminder of your commitment to personal and spiritual development, empowering you to overcome obstacles and embrace opportunities for growth with courage and confidence.

20. SUNRISE MEDITATION SPELL

Ingredients:
- A quiet and serene outdoor space or a room with a view of the sunrise
- Comfortable clothing
- A blanket or cushion for sitting

Preparation:
1. Choose a location where you can comfortably view the sunrise without distractions. This could be a balcony, garden, or simply a room with a window facing east.
2. Settle into the space a few minutes before sunrise. Arrange your cushion or blanket for comfort.

Spell Instructions:
1. Set Your Intention:
   - Close your eyes and take a few deep breaths to center yourself.
   - Set your intention for the sunrise meditation: to embrace the new day as an opportunity for growth, renewal, and transformation.

2. Witness the Sunrise:
   - As the first light of dawn begins to illuminate the

sky, open your eyes and gaze towards the horizon.
- Watch as the sun slowly rises above the horizon, filling the sky with vibrant colors and warmth.

3. Connect with the Energy:
- Feel the energy of the rising sun permeating your being. Visualize its rays filling you with vitality, strength, and positivity.
- As you bask in the glow of the sunrise, feel a sense of renewal and rejuvenation washing over you.

4. Visualize Growth and Opportunities:
- With your eyes closed, visualize the new day unfolding before you like a blank canvas, brimming with infinite possibilities for growth and expansion.
- See yourself stepping forward into the day with confidence, embracing challenges as opportunities for learning and transformation.

5. Express Gratitude:
- Take a moment to express gratitude for the beauty of the sunrise and the gift of a new day.
- Thank the universe for the opportunities it presents for growth, renewal, and self-discovery.

6. Close the Meditation:
- When you feel ready, gently bring your awareness back to the present moment.
- Take a few deep breaths and slowly open your eyes, feeling refreshed and energized by the experience.

Additional Tips:
- You can enhance your sunrise meditation by incorporating gentle movement or stretching exercises to awaken your body and mind.
- Consider keeping a journal nearby to jot down any insights or inspirations that arise during your meditation.
- Repeat this sunrise meditation ritual regularly to deepen your connection with the energy of the sunrise and harness its transformative power for personal growth and renewal.

By engaging in this Sunrise Meditation Spell, you align yourself with the energy of the rising sun and set the stage for a day filled with growth, opportunity, and renewal. As you embrace each new day with mindfulness and intention, you empower yourself to step into your fullest potential and embrace the journey of self-discovery and transformation.

21. POSITIVE LETTER TO SELF SPELL

Ingredients:
- Pen and paper or a digital device for writing
- A quiet and comfortable space

Preparation:
1. Find a quiet and comfortable space where you can focus without distractions.
2. Set aside a few minutes to clear your mind and center yourself.

Spell Instructions:
1. Set Your Intention:
   - Take a few deep breaths to center yourself and focus your attention on the present moment.
   - Set your intention for this spell: to express love, pride, and encouragement to yourself as you reflect on your growth journey.

2. Write Your Letter:
   - Begin writing your letter to yourself, addressing it with words of affection and encouragement.
   - Reflect on your personal growth and achievements, acknowledging the challenges you've overcome and the progress you've made.

- Express pride in your accomplishments, no matter how big or small, and celebrate the steps you've taken towards becoming the best version of yourself.

3. Encourage Continued Development:
    - Encourage yourself to continue on your path of growth and self-discovery, emphasizing the importance of self-compassion, self-care, and resilience.
  - Offer words of wisdom and guidance, reminding yourself of your inherent worth and the limitless potential within you.

4. Read It Often:
  - Once your letter is complete, keep it in a place where you can easily access it, such as a journal, notebook, or digital device.
  - Commit to reading your letter to yourself regularly, whether it's daily, weekly, or whenever you need a boost of positivity and encouragement.

Additional Tips:
- Personalize your letter with specific examples of growth and achievements that are meaningful to you.
- Consider adding affirmations or mantras that resonate with your goals and aspirations to further amplify the spell's effects.
- Use this positive letter as a tool for self-reflection and empowerment, allowing it to serve as a constant source of inspiration and motivation on your journey of personal growth and development.

By engaging in this Positive Letter to Self Spell, you harness the power of self-love, encouragement, and affirmation to nurture your growth journey and cultivate a positive mindset. Each time you read your letter, let it remind you of your strengths, resilience, and potential, empowering you to continue moving forward with confidence and determination.

22. HERBAL SACHET SPELL FOR GROWTH AND CLARITY

Ingredients:
- Sachet or small pouch
- Dried rosemary
- Dried sage
- Dried mint
- A quiet and focused space

Preparation:
1. Find a quiet and comfortable space where you can focus without distractions.
2. Set aside a few minutes to clear your mind and center yourself.

Spell Instructions:
1. Set Your Intention:
   - Close your eyes and take a few deep breaths to center yourself.
   - Set your intention for this spell: to infuse the herbal sachet with energies of growth, clarity, and inspiration.

2. Fill the Sachet:

- Open the sachet or pouch and begin filling it with dried rosemary, sage, and mint.
- As you add each herb, visualize it imbued with the qualities you wish to cultivate—rosemary for mental clarity, sage for wisdom and guidance, and mint for inspiration and growth.

3. Seal the Sachet:
- Once the sachet is filled with herbs, gently close it and tie it securely with a knot or ribbon.
- Take a moment to hold the sachet in your hands and infuse it with your intention, focusing your energy on imbuing it with the qualities of growth and clarity.

4. Place Near Your Workspace:
- Keep the herbal sachet near your workspace —a desk, workstation, or wherever you engage in activities that require focus and clarity.
- You can place it in a drawer, on a shelf, or simply keep it nearby where you can see or touch it regularly.

Additional Tips:
- Consider adding other herbs or botanicals that resonate with your intentions for growth and clarity, such as lavender for calmness or lemon balm for mental clarity.
- Refresh the herbal sachet periodically by gently crushing the herbs to release their aroma and energy.
- Use the sachet as a focal point for meditation or visualization exercises, holding it in your hands and connecting with its energy to enhance your focus and

clarity.

By creating and using this Herbal Sachet Spell, you harness the energies of rosemary, sage, and mint to inspire growth, clarity, and inspiration in your workspace. Allow the herbal sachet to serve as a potent reminder of your intentions and a source of support as you navigate your journey of personal and professional development.

23. DAILY GRATITUDE RITUAL SPELL

Ingredients:
- Journal or notebook
- Pen or pencil
- A quiet and comfortable space

Preparation:
1. Find a quiet and comfortable space where you can focus without distractions.
2. Set aside a few minutes before bedtime to engage in this ritual.

Spell Instructions:
1. Set Your Intention:
   - Close your eyes and take a few deep breaths to center yourself.
   - Set your intention for this ritual: to cultivate gratitude and reflection by acknowledging the blessings and lessons of the day.

2. Reflect on Your Day:
   - Open your journal or notebook and begin reflecting on the events of the day.
   - Think about three things you learned or experienced that day—big or small—and take a

moment to appreciate them.

3. Express Gratitude:
   - Write down each of the three things you learned or experienced, followed by a statement of gratitude.
   - Reflect on why each of these things is meaningful to you and how it has enriched your life in some way.

4. Close with a Positive Affirmation:
   - End each entry with a positive affirmation or statement of intention for the next day.
   - This could be a declaration of self-love, a commitment to growth, or simply a reminder to stay present and grateful.

5. Repeat Daily:
   - Commit to engaging in this gratitude ritual every night before bed.
   - Make it a regular part of your evening routine, allowing it to become a sacred space for reflection and appreciation.

Additional Tips:
- Consider adding creative touches to your gratitude journal, such as drawings, stickers, or colorful markers, to make it more visually appealing and engaging.
- Experiment with different prompts or variations of the ritual, such as focusing on specific themes or areas of gratitude each night.
- Share your gratitude journal with a friend, partner,

or loved one to deepen your connection and inspire each other's gratitude practice.

By engaging in this Daily Gratitude Ritual Spell, you create a powerful space for reflection, appreciation, and mindfulness in your daily life. As you cultivate a habit of gratitude and reflection, you open yourself up to the abundance of blessings and lessons that surround you, fostering a deeper sense of joy, fulfillment, and connection with the world around you.

24. GROWTH MINDSET CANDLE SPELL

Ingredients:
- Candle (preferably in a color that resonates with growth and renewal, such as green or yellow)
- Matches or a lighter
- A quiet and focused space

Preparation:
1. Find a quiet and comfortable space where you can focus without distractions.
2. Set aside a few minutes to clear your mind and center yourself.

Spell Instructions:
1. Set Your Intention:
   - Close your eyes and take a few deep breaths to center yourself.
   - Set your intention for this spell: to cultivate a growth mindset and embrace the power of positive affirmations.

2. Prepare the Candle:
   - Place the candle in front of you on a stable surface.
   - Take a moment to hold the candle in your hands and visualize it filling with energy and light,

representing your growth mindset.

3. Light the Candle:
   - Using matches or a lighter, carefully light the candle.
   - As you do so, imagine the flame igniting the spark of growth and potential within you.

4. Focus on the Flame:
   - Gaze at the flame of the candle and let it draw your attention.
   - Allow yourself to become fully present in the moment, focusing your thoughts and intentions on the candle's flame.

5. Repeat Growth Affirmations:
   - While gazing at the flame, repeat positive affirmations related to growth and resilience.
   - Affirmations could include statements such as "I embrace challenges as opportunities for growth," "I am capable of learning and evolving," and "I believe in my ability to overcome obstacles."

6. Visualize Your Growth:
   - As you repeat the affirmations, visualize yourself expanding and flourishing, like a seedling reaching towards the sun.
   - See yourself overcoming challenges with ease and embracing new opportunities for learning and development.

7. Express Gratitude:
   - Take a moment to express gratitude for the growth mindset you are cultivating and for the opportunities that lie ahead.
   - Thank the universe for its support and guidance on your journey of personal and spiritual growth.

8. Close the Ritual:
   - When you feel ready, slowly extinguish the candle flame with a candle snuffer or by gently blowing it out.
   - Take a few deep breaths and ground yourself in the present moment, feeling the energy of the ritual imbuing your being.

Additional Tips:
- You can enhance the ritual by incorporating other elements that resonate with growth and renewal, such as crystals like green aventurine or citrine, or essential oils like rosemary or lemon.
- Repeat this Growth Mindset Candle Spell regularly to reinforce your commitment to growth and resilience, especially during times of challenge or uncertainty.
- Keep the candle in a prominent place as a reminder of your dedication to cultivating a growth mindset and embracing the journey of personal and spiritual development.

Through the practice of this Growth Mindset Candle Spell, you empower yourself to embrace challenges, cultivate resilience, and unlock your full potential for growth and transformation. May the flame of the candle serve as a beacon of inspiration and guidance on your journey towards a more empowered and fulfilling life.

25. NATURE MEDITATION SPELL

Ingredients:
- A natural outdoor setting such as a forest, park, beach, or garden
- Comfortable clothing suitable for the weather
- Optional: A blanket or cushion for sitting

Preparation:
1. Choose a natural outdoor location that resonates with you and offers a sense of tranquility and connection to nature.
2. Dress comfortably for the weather and consider bringing along any additional items like a blanket or cushion for sitting.

Spell Instructions:
1. Set Your Intention:
   - As you enter the outdoor space, take a moment to connect with the energy of nature around you.
   - Set your intention for this meditation: to connect with the natural world and gain insights into your own growth and life journey.

2. Find a Comfortable Spot:
   - Explore the area and find a comfortable spot to sit or

lie down where you feel safe and supported.
- If possible, choose a spot where you can easily observe the natural surroundings, such as under a tree or near a body of water.

3. Connect with Your Breath:
- Close your eyes and take several deep breaths, allowing yourself to relax and become fully present in the moment.
- Notice the sensation of the air filling your lungs and the gentle rhythm of your breath.

4. Observe Your Surroundings:
- With your eyes still closed or softly open, begin to observe the sights, sounds, and sensations of the natural environment around you.
- Notice the movement of the leaves in the breeze, the sound of birdsong, the warmth of the sun on your skin, and any other sensory experiences that arise.

5. Meditate on Growth and Renewal:
- As you continue to immerse yourself in the natural surroundings, reflect on the processes of growth and renewal that occur in the natural world.
- Consider how plants sprout from seeds, trees grow tall and strong, and seasons change in a continuous cycle of birth, growth, death, and rebirth.

6. Connect with Your Own Growth Journey:
- As you contemplate the natural growth processes, reflect on your own life journey and personal growth.

- Consider the challenges you've faced, the lessons you've learned, and the ways in which you've grown and evolved over time.

7. Express Gratitude:
 - Take a moment to express gratitude for the natural world and the wisdom it offers.
 - Thank the earth, the elements, and the plants and animals for their presence and the lessons they impart.

8. Close the Meditation:
 - When you feel ready, gently bring your awareness back to your breath and the sensations of your body.
 - Slowly open your eyes and take in your surroundings, feeling refreshed and rejuvenated by your connection with nature.

Additional Tips:
- You can enhance your nature meditation by incorporating other elements such as grounding exercises, visualization techniques, or mindfulness practices.
- Consider bringing along a journal to record any insights, inspirations, or reflections that arise during your meditation.
- Repeat this nature meditation ritual regularly to deepen your connection with the natural world and gain new perspectives on your own growth and life journey.

Through the practice of this Nature Meditation Spell, you align yourself with the rhythms of the natural world and tap into its inherent wisdom and energy. May your time spent in nature inspire you, nurture your spirit, and guide you on your path of growth and transformation.

26. SELF-CARE DAY SPELL

Ingredients:
- A day set aside for self-care activities
- A list of self-care activities that nourish your mind, body, and spirit
- Optional: Candles, essential oils, calming music, or any other items that enhance relaxation

Preparation:
1. Choose a day when you can fully dedicate yourself to self-care activities without interruptions or obligations.
2. Create a list of self-care activities that resonate with you and address your mental, physical, and emotional well-being.

Spell Instructions:
1. Set Your Intention:
   - Begin your self-care day by setting a clear intention for nourishing your mind, body, and spirit.
   - Visualize yourself embracing each activity with presence, intention, and gratitude for the opportunity to care for yourself.

2. Choose Your Activities:
   - Review your list of self-care activities and choose

the ones that you feel drawn to and that will best support your needs on this day.

- Consider a mix of activities that nurture your physical body, engage your mind, and uplift your spirit.

3. Create a Sacred Space:
- Prepare a quiet and comfortable space where you can engage in your self-care activities without distractions.
- Light candles, diffuse essential oils, or play calming music to enhance the atmosphere and promote relaxation.

4. Engage in Self-Care Activities:
- Begin your self-care day by engaging in the activities you've chosen, one at a time or as part of a fluid and intuitive flow.
- Focus on fully immersing yourself in each activity, savoring the sensations, and allowing yourself to be present in the moment.

5. Nourish Your Body:
- Dedicate time to nourishing your physical body through activities such as gentle exercise, healthy meals, relaxation techniques, or pampering rituals like baths or massages.

6. Nurture Your Mind:
- Engage your mind in activities that stimulate creativity, learning, or relaxation, such as reading,

journaling, practicing mindfulness, or engaging in a creative hobby.

7. Uplift Your Spirit:
 - Cultivate feelings of joy, gratitude, and connection by engaging in activities that uplift your spirit, such as spending time in nature, practicing gratitude, meditating, or connecting with loved ones.

8. Express Gratitude:
 - Throughout your self-care day, take moments to express gratitude for the opportunity to care for yourself and nourish your well-being.
 - Reflect on the abundance of blessings in your life and the importance of prioritizing self-care as a form of self-love and empowerment.

9. Close the Day with Reflection:
 - As your self-care day comes to a close, take time to reflect on your experiences and how each activity has contributed to your overall sense of well-being and growth.
 - Express gratitude for the day's nourishment and set an intention to carry the energy of self-care forward in your daily life.

Additional Tips:
- Customize your self-care day to align with your unique needs, preferences, and interests.
- Consider inviting a friend or loved one to join you for part of your self-care day, enhancing the sense of

connection and support.
- Repeat this self-care day ritual regularly to prioritize your well-being and foster a deeper sense of self-love and empowerment.

Through the practice of this Self-Care Day Spell, you honor your inherent worth and prioritize your well-being, nurturing your mind, body, and spirit in a sacred and intentional way. May your self-care day be a source of replenishment, rejuvenation, and growth, empowering you to thrive in all areas of your life.

27. GRATITUDE JAR SPELL

Ingredients:
- A jar or container
- Small slips of paper
- Pen or pencil

Preparation:
1. Find a jar or container that resonates with you and feels special.
2. Cut small slips of paper that will fit inside the jar.
3. Place the jar and slips of paper in a prominent and easily accessible location.

Spell Instructions:
1. Set Your Intention:
   - Begin by setting a clear intention for your gratitude jar: to cultivate a mindset of appreciation for your accomplishments and growth experiences.

2. Write Your Gratitude Notes:
   - Each time you achieve an accomplishment or have a positive growth experience, take a moment to reflect on it.
   - Write down the accomplishment or experience on a slip of paper, expressing gratitude for the opportunity to grow and learn.

3. Add to the Jar:
   - Fold the slip of paper and place it inside the gratitude jar.
   - As you do so, visualize the energy of gratitude infusing the jar, filling it with positivity and abundance.

4. Review Regularly:
   - Set aside time regularly to review the slips of paper in your gratitude jar.
   - Take out each slip and reflect on the accomplishment or growth experience it represents.
   - Allow yourself to fully appreciate and celebrate your progress and achievements.

5. Express Gratitude:
   - As you review each slip of paper, take a moment to express gratitude for the growth and learning it represents.
   - Acknowledge the effort and dedication you've put into your personal and spiritual development.

6. Set New Intentions:
   - After reviewing the slips of paper, take a moment to set new intentions for your continued growth and development.
   - Visualize yourself achieving new goals and experiencing further growth and success.

7. Repeat Regularly:

- Make a habit of adding to and reviewing your gratitude jar regularly, whether it's daily, weekly, or monthly.
   - Consistency is key to deepening your sense of gratitude and appreciation for your journey of growth.

Additional Tips:
- Decorate your gratitude jar to make it visually appealing and inspiring.
- Consider incorporating affirmations or quotes about gratitude and growth into your jar's design.
- Share your gratitude jar practice with friends or loved ones to inspire them to cultivate their own mindset of appreciation.

Through the practice of this Gratitude Jar Spell, you create a tangible and powerful tool for fostering a mindset of appreciation and celebration for your accomplishments and growth experiences. May your gratitude jar serve as a constant reminder of your progress and potential, inspiring you to continue striving for growth and fulfillment in all areas of your life.

28. AFFIRMATION MIRROR SPELL

Ingredients:
- Sticky notes or small pieces of paper
- Pen or marker

Preparation:
1. Gather sticky notes or small pieces of paper and a pen or marker.
2. Choose affirmations that resonate with your desire for growth and empowerment.

Spell Instructions:
1. Set Your Intention:
    - Begin by setting a clear intention for your affirmation mirror: to cultivate a mindset of growth and empowerment each day.

2. Write Your Affirmations:
   - Write down growth-oriented affirmations on the sticky notes or small pieces of paper.
   - Choose affirmations that inspire and uplift you, reinforcing your belief in your abilities and potential for growth.

3. Place Affirmations on Your Mirror:

- Stick the affirmations onto your mirror, arranging them in a way that is visually pleasing and easily accessible.
- As you place each affirmation, visualize the mirror becoming a reflection of your inner strength and determination.

4. Read Aloud Each Day:
   - Each day, take a moment to stand in front of your mirror and read the affirmations aloud to yourself.
   - Speak the affirmations with conviction and belief, allowing their empowering words to resonate deeply within you.

5. Embody the Affirmations:
   - As you read each affirmation, take a moment to embody its message.
   - Visualize yourself embracing growth, overcoming challenges, and stepping into your fullest potential.

6. Express Gratitude:
   - After reading the affirmations, take a moment to express gratitude for the growth and empowerment they bring into your life.
   - Acknowledge the power of positive self-talk in shaping your mindset and experiences.

7. Repeat Daily:
   - Make it a daily ritual to read the affirmations on your mirror, ideally in the morning to set a positive tone for the day ahead.

- Consistency is key to reinforcing the empowering beliefs and attitudes contained within the affirmations.

Additional Tips:
- Experiment with different affirmations to find ones that resonate most deeply with you and your goals.
- Consider adding new affirmations or rotating existing ones periodically to keep your practice fresh and inspiring.
- Share your affirmation mirror practice with friends or loved ones to inspire them to cultivate their own mindset of growth and empowerment.

Through the practice of this Affirmation Mirror Spell, you harness the power of positive self-talk to cultivate a mindset of growth, empowerment, and belief in your unlimited potential. May the affirmations on your mirror serve as daily reminders of your strength, resilience, and capacity for personal transformation.

29. VISUALIZATION WALK SPELL

Ingredients:
- A quiet outdoor space conducive to walking
- Comfortable walking shoes
- Optional: A journal or recording device for reflection

Preparation:
1. Choose a time and location for your visualization walk where you can walk undisturbed and connect with nature.
2. Dress comfortably for the weather and wear supportive walking shoes.

Spell Instructions:
1. Set Your Intention:
   - Begin by setting a clear intention for your visualization walk: to visualize yourself successfully overcoming challenges and growing stronger.

2. Enter the Outdoor Space:
   - Enter the outdoor space and take a moment to connect with the natural surroundings.
   - Feel the earth beneath your feet, the breeze on your skin, and the sounds of nature around you.

3. Begin Walking:
 - Start walking at a comfortable pace, allowing your body to move rhythmically with each step.
  - Focus on your breath and the sensation of movement as you traverse the outdoor environment.

4. Engage in Visualization:
  - As you walk, begin to engage in visualization by imagining yourself successfully overcoming challenges and growing stronger.
  - Picture yourself facing obstacles with courage and determination, finding creative solutions, and emerging victorious.

5. Use All Your Senses:
 - Engage all your senses in the visualization process. Notice the sights, sounds, smells, and sensations associated with your imagined success.
  - Feel the satisfaction and empowerment that comes from overcoming challenges and achieving your goals.

6. Express Gratitude:
 - Throughout your visualization walk, take moments to express gratitude for your ability to visualize success and growth.
  - Acknowledge the power of your imagination and the potential it holds for shaping your reality.

7. Reflect and Integrate:
  - After completing your visualization walk, take a

few moments to reflect on your experience.
 - Consider jotting down any insights or inspirations that arose during the walk in a journal or recording them for later reflection.

8. Repeat Regularly:
 - Make visualization walks a regular practice in your routine, ideally incorporating them into your daily or weekly schedule.
 - Consistency is key to harnessing the full benefits of visualization for personal growth and empowerment.

Additional Tips:
- Experiment with different environments for your visualization walks, such as forests, parks, or coastal areas, to tap into different energies and inspirations.
- If you prefer, you can listen to calming music or guided visualizations during your walk to enhance the experience.
- Share your visualization walk practice with friends or loved ones to inspire them to cultivate their own mindset of success and growth.

Through the practice of this Visualization Walk Spell, you harness the power of visualization to envision yourself overcoming challenges and growing stronger. May each step you take on your visualization walks bring you closer to the realization of your goals and aspirations, empowering you to thrive in all areas of your life.

30. GROWTH SIGIL MEDITATION SPELL

Ingredients:
- A quiet and comfortable meditation space
- A sigil representing growth (hand-drawn or printed)
- Optional: Incense, candles, or calming music to enhance the meditation experience

Preparation:
1. Find a quiet and comfortable space where you can sit or lie down without distractions.
2. Have your growth sigil ready, whether it's hand-drawn on paper or digitally created.

Spell Instructions:
1. Set Your Intention:
   - Begin by setting a clear intention for your growth sigil meditation: to harness the power of the sigil to empower your personal growth journey.

2. Prepare Your Space:
   - Light candles, burn incense, or play calming music if desired to create a soothing atmosphere conducive to meditation.
   - Sit or lie down in a comfortable position, ensuring that your spine is straight and your body is relaxed.

3. Focus on the Sigil:
 - Take a few deep breaths to center yourself and clear your mind.
 - Gaze upon the growth sigil before you, allowing your eyes to focus on its lines, shapes, and symbols.

4. Visualize Empowerment:
 - Close your eyes and visualize the growth sigil glowing with a radiant energy that fills the space around you.
 - Envision the sigil's energy flowing into your being, infusing you with a sense of empowerment, strength, and determination.

5. Connect with Your Intentions:
 - As you meditate on the growth sigil, connect with your intentions for personal growth and development.
 - Visualize yourself overcoming obstacles, embracing challenges, and stepping into your fullest potential with confidence and grace.

6. Repeat Affirmations:
 - Repeat affirmations or mantras related to growth and empowerment silently or aloud as you meditate.
 - Allow the positive affirmations to reinforce your belief in your ability to grow and evolve in all areas of your life.

7. Express Gratitude:

- Throughout the meditation, express gratitude for the opportunity to embark on a journey of growth and self-discovery.
  - Acknowledge the support of the sigil and the universe in guiding you along your path.

8. Close the Meditation:
  - When you feel ready, gently bring your awareness back to your surroundings.
  - Thank the growth sigil for its energy and guidance, knowing that its empowering influence will continue to support you on your journey.

Additional Tips:
- Experiment with different meditation techniques, such as breathwork or visualization, to enhance your experience with the growth sigil.
- Keep a journal nearby to record any insights, inspirations, or messages that arise during the meditation.
- Use the growth sigil meditation regularly to reinforce your commitment to personal growth and to amplify its effects over time.

Through the practice of this Growth Sigil Meditation Spell, you tap into the transformative power of your sigil to empower your personal growth journey. May each meditation session bring you closer to realizing your fullest potential and experiencing profound growth in all aspects of your life.

31. LEARNING CIRCLE SPELL

Ingredients:
- A group of friends, colleagues, or like-minded individuals
- A comfortable and inviting space for gathering
- Optional: Refreshments or snacks to enjoy during the circle

Preparation:
1. Choose a date, time, and location for your learning circle gathering.
2. Invite friends, colleagues, or individuals who share your interest in personal growth and learning.
3. Set the intention for the circle to be a supportive and nurturing space for sharing knowledge and experiences.

Spell Instructions:
1. Gather in Circle:
   - Assemble with your group in a circle formation, ensuring everyone has a clear view and can easily engage in conversation.
   - Take a moment to center yourselves and connect with the energy of the circle.

2. Share Your Learnings:
- Begin the circle by inviting each participant to share something they've learned recently or a way in which they've grown.
- Encourage everyone to speak from the heart and share openly, without fear of judgment.

3. Listen with Presence:
- As each person shares, listen attentively and with an open heart.
- Offer supportive nods, smiles, and affirmations to show your appreciation for their contribution.

4. Reflect and Discuss:
- After each person has shared, take time for reflection and discussion.
- Encourage participants to ask questions, offer insights, and engage in meaningful dialogue about the topics shared.

5. Express Gratitude:
- Express gratitude for the opportunity to learn from each other and grow together.
- Take a moment to acknowledge the wisdom and unique perspectives that each individual brings to the circle.

6. Set Intentions for Growth:
- Conclude the circle by setting intentions for continued growth and learning.
- Encourage participants to commit to taking action

based on the insights gained during the circle.

7. Close the Circle:
   - Close the circle by joining hands or sharing a collective affirmation of unity and support.
   - Thank each participant for their presence and contributions to the learning circle.

Additional Tips:
- Consider establishing a regular schedule for your learning circle gatherings, such as monthly or quarterly meetings, to maintain momentum and foster deeper connections.
- Rotate facilitators or discussion topics to ensure a diverse range of perspectives and experiences are shared within the circle.
- Encourage participants to take notes or journal about their experiences during the circle and any insights gained for further reflection.

Through the practice of this Learning Circle Spell, you create a sacred space for sharing knowledge, experiences, and insights with others who are also on a journey of growth and learning. May each gathering bring new perspectives, inspiration, and opportunities for personal and collective growth.

32. POSITIVE SELF-TALK RITUAL SPELL

Ingredients:
- Quiet and comfortable space for reflection
- Optional: Candle, incense, or calming music to enhance the ambiance

Preparation:
1. Choose a consistent time each day to dedicate to your positive self-talk ritual.
2. Find a quiet and comfortable space where you can be alone and undisturbed.

Spell Instructions:
1. Set Your Intention:
   - Begin by setting a clear intention for your positive self-talk ritual: to speak kindly and encouragingly to yourself, focusing on your growth and development.

2. Create a Peaceful Atmosphere:
   - Light a candle, burn incense, or play calming music if desired to create a soothing and sacred ambiance for your ritual.
   - Sit or stand in a comfortable position, allowing yourself to relax and unwind.

3. Speak Kindly to Yourself:
   - Start speaking aloud or silently to yourself, using words of kindness, encouragement, and affirmation.
   - Acknowledge your strengths, achievements, and progress, no matter how small.

4. Focus on Growth:
   - Direct your self-talk towards areas of growth and development, affirming your ability to learn, adapt, and overcome challenges.
   - Repeat affirmations related to your personal goals, aspirations, and desires for growth.

5. Visualize Success:
   - Close your eyes and visualize yourself achieving your goals, overcoming obstacles, and stepping into your fullest potential.
   - Immerse yourself in the feelings of confidence, empowerment, and fulfillment that accompany your envisioned success.

6. Express Gratitude:
   - Take a moment to express gratitude for your journey of growth and the opportunities for self-improvement that lie ahead.
   - Appreciate yourself for your efforts, resilience, and commitment to personal development.

7. Seal Your Intentions:
   - Conclude the ritual by reaffirming your intentions for positive self-talk and growth.

- Commit to continuing this practice daily, knowing that each moment of self-affirmation brings you closer to your highest potential.

Additional Tips:
- Personalize your positive self-talk ritual by incorporating specific affirmations or mantras that resonate with your goals and aspirations.
- Keep a journal nearby to jot down any insights, reflections, or breakthroughs that arise during your ritual.
- Share your positive self-talk practice with trusted friends or loved ones to inspire them to cultivate a mindset of self-love and growth.

Through the practice of this Positive Self-Talk Ritual Spell, you harness the power of your words to uplift, motivate, and empower yourself on your journey of growth and self-discovery. May each moment of self-affirmation bring you closer to realizing your fullest potential and living a life filled with joy, fulfillment, and abundance.

33. LEARNING ALTAR SPELL

Ingredients:
- A small table or shelf to serve as your altar
- Items representing knowledge, growth, and learning:
  - Books or scrolls
  - Symbols of wisdom (such as an owl figurine)
  - Crystals associated with learning and mental clarity (like clear quartz or fluorite)
  - Plants or herbs associated with intellect and growth (such as sage or rosemary)
  - Personal items related to your own learning journey (like notebooks, pens, or mementos from educational experiences)
- Optional: Candle, incense, or other altar decorations to enhance the ambiance

Preparation:
1. Choose a designated space in your home where you can set up your learning altar. Ensure it's a quiet and undisturbed area where you can focus and reflect.
2. Gather the items you've chosen to represent knowledge, growth, and learning.

Spell Instructions:

1. Set Your Intention:
   - Begin by setting a clear intention for your learning altar: to create a sacred space dedicated to your growth and development through learning.

2. Arrange Your Altar:
   - Place your chosen items on the altar in a way that feels visually pleasing and meaningful to you.
   - Consider arranging them in a way that symbolizes the journey of learning, with items flowing from beginner's knowledge to deeper wisdom.

3. Invoke Learning Energies:
   - Light a candle or burn incense to cleanse and consecrate the space, invoking energies of wisdom, clarity, and growth.
   - Visualize the altar becoming a focal point for learning energies, attracting inspiration and insights to support your educational journey.

4. Spend Time in Reflection:
   - Daily, spend time at your learning altar, reflecting on your learning journey and aspirations.
   - Meditate on the items on your altar, allowing their symbolism to inspire and motivate you in your pursuit of knowledge.

5. Set Learning Intentions:
   - While at your altar, set intentions for your learning goals and the areas of knowledge you wish to explore or deepen.

- Speak your intentions aloud or silently, infusing them with the energy of the altar and your own determination to grow.

6. Express Gratitude:
  - Express gratitude for the opportunity to learn and grow, acknowledging the blessings of knowledge and wisdom in your life.
  - Thank the items on your altar for their presence and the inspiration they provide on your learning journey.

7. Close Your Practice:
   - When you're ready to leave your altar, take a moment to ground yourself and integrate the insights gained during your reflection.
   - Leave the altar feeling uplifted and inspired, knowing that it will continue to support and guide you on your path of learning and growth.

 Additional Tips:
- Keep your learning altar clean and tidy, periodically dusting and rearranging the items to maintain its sacred energy.
- Feel free to add or remove items from your altar as your learning journey evolves and new interests arise.
- Invite friends or study partners to join you at your learning altar for group study sessions or discussions, harnessing the collective energy for mutual growth.

Through the practice of this Learning Altar Spell, you

create a sacred space dedicated to your growth and development through learning. May your altar serve as a source of inspiration, wisdom, and guidance on your educational journey, empowering you to unlock new levels of knowledge and understanding in all areas of your life.

34. CRYSTAL INFUSED WATER SPELL

Ingredients:
- Clear quartz crystal
- Glass or jar of water

Preparation:
1. Choose a clear quartz crystal that resonates with you and your intention for fostering a growth mindset.
2. Fill a glass or jar with water, ensuring it's clean and free from impurities.

Spell Instructions:
1. Set Your Intention:
   - Hold the clear quartz crystal in your hands and set your intention for fostering a growth mindset.
   - Visualize yourself embracing new opportunities, expanding your knowledge, and overcoming challenges with resilience and determination.

2. Charge the Water:
   - Place the clear quartz crystal in the glass or jar of water, ensuring it's fully submerged.
   - Leave the crystal-infused water to sit overnight, allowing the energy of the crystal to imbue the water

with its properties.

3. Morning Ritual:
- In the morning, retrieve the glass or jar of crystal-infused water.
- Hold the container in your hands and take a few deep breaths to center yourself.

4. Drink with Intentions:
- As you drink the crystal-infused water, focus on your intention for fostering a growth mindset.
- Visualize the water flowing through your body, carrying with it the energy of the clear quartz crystal and amplifying your commitment to growth and expansion.

5. Affirmations:
- Repeat affirmations aloud or silently as you drink the water, reinforcing your intentions for personal growth and development.
- Affirm statements such as "I embrace challenges as opportunities for growth" or "I am open to learning and expanding my horizons."

6. Express Gratitude:
- Take a moment to express gratitude for the nourishment and energy provided by the crystal-infused water.
- Thank the clear quartz crystal for its support in your journey toward a growth mindset.

7. Integrate the Energy:
   - Carry the energy of the crystal-infused water with you throughout the day, allowing it to remind you of your commitment to growth and expansion.
   - Remain open to new experiences, insights, and opportunities for learning that may arise.

Additional Tips:
- You can enhance the potency of the spell by placing the glass or jar of crystal-infused water on your altar or in a sacred space overnight.
- Experiment with different crystals to infuse your water with specific energies that support your growth mindset, such as citrine for abundance or amethyst for intuition.
- Regularly replenish your supply of crystal-infused water to maintain a continuous flow of energy and intention.

Through the practice of this Crystal Infused Water Spell, you align yourself with the energies of growth and expansion, harnessing the power of clear quartz crystal to support your journey toward a mindset of continual learning and development. May each sip of crystal-infused water nourish your soul and inspire you to reach new heights of personal and spiritual growth.

35. SUNLIGHT MEDITATION SPELL

Ingredients:
- A comfortable and sunny spot to sit or lie down

Spell Instructions:
1. Choose Your Space:
   - Find a comfortable spot where you can bask in the sunlight without distractions. This could be a sunny patch in your garden, a balcony, or near a window where the sunlight streams in.

2. Prepare Yourself:
   - Sit or lie down in a relaxed position, allowing your body to settle into a comfortable posture.
   - Take a few deep breaths to center yourself and clear your mind of any distractions.

3. Connect with the Sunlight:
   - Close your eyes and turn your face toward the sunlight, feeling its warmth on your skin.
   - Visualize the sunlight as a radiant golden energy, filling the space around you with its vibrant light and warmth.

4. Set Your Intention:

- Focus your attention inward and set your intention for the meditation. Affirm your desire to harness the energy of the sunlight for growth and vitality.

5. Visualize Growth and Vitality:
   - With each breath, visualize the sunlight streaming into your body, infusing every cell with energy and vitality.
   - Imagine this golden light expanding within you, nourishing your spirit and awakening your inner potential for growth and development.

6. Embrace the Energy:
   - Allow yourself to bask in the sunlight's energy, feeling it uplift your mood, invigorate your spirit, and inspire you to reach new heights.
   - Embrace the warmth and brightness of the sunlight, knowing that it is fueling your journey toward growth and expansion.

7. Express Gratitude:
   - Take a moment to express gratitude for the life-giving energy of the sun and the opportunity to connect with its power.
   - Thank the sunlight for its support in your journey toward personal and spiritual growth.

8. Close the Meditation:
   - When you feel ready, gently bring your awareness back to your surroundings.
   - Open your eyes and take a few more deep breaths,

feeling grounded and revitalized by the sunlight meditation.

Additional Tips:
- You can enhance the potency of the sunlight meditation by incorporating affirmations or mantras related to growth and vitality.
- Practice this meditation regularly, ideally during the morning when the sunlight is most abundant and energizing.
- Experiment with different positions and postures to find what feels most comfortable and conducive to deep relaxation and connection with the sunlight.

Through the practice of this Sunlight Meditation Spell, you tap into the life-giving energy of the sun, harnessing its power to fuel your journey toward growth, vitality, and personal transformation. May each moment spent in the sunlight fill you with renewed energy, inspiration, and a deep sense of connection to the cycles of nature and the limitless potential within you.

36. DAILY LEARNING CARD SPELL

Ingredients:
- Tarot deck or oracle cards

Spell Instructions:
1. Prepare Your Space:
   - Find a quiet and comfortable space where you can focus on your daily card drawing ritual. Light a candle or some incense if desired to create a sacred atmosphere.

2. Center Yourself:
   - Take a few deep breaths to center yourself and clear your mind of any distractions. Ground yourself by connecting with the energy of the earth beneath you.

3. Set Your Intention:
   - Hold the deck of tarot or oracle cards in your hands and set your intention for the reading. Affirm your desire to receive guidance and insights related to your learning and growth journey.

4. Shuffle the Cards:
   - Shuffle the cards while focusing on your intention. Visualize the energy of learning and growth infusing

the cards with wisdom and clarity.

5. Draw Your Daily Card:
   - When you feel ready, draw a single card from the deck. Trust your intuition and allow the card to choose you, knowing that it holds a message specifically for your learning and growth.

6. Reflect on the Card:
   - Examine the imagery and symbolism of the card you've drawn. Notice any thoughts, feelings, or insights that arise as you study the card.

7. Interpret the Message:
   - Reflect on the message of the card in the context of your learning journey. Consider how its themes relate to your current experiences, challenges, and goals.

8. Journal Your Insights:
   - Take a few moments to journal about the card and the insights it has sparked. Write down any revelations, epiphanies, or action steps that come to mind.

9. Express Gratitude:
   - Express gratitude for the guidance and wisdom you've received through the daily card reading. Thank the cards for their role in supporting your learning and growth.

10. Carry the Message with You:

- Throughout the day, carry the message of the card with you as a source of inspiration and guidance. Allow its wisdom to inform your decisions and actions.

Additional Tips:
- You can enhance the potency of this spell by incorporating crystals or other divination tools into your daily card drawing ritual.
- Keep a journal dedicated to recording your daily card readings and the insights they inspire. Reviewing your journal entries over time can provide valuable perspective on your learning and growth journey.
- Experiment with different tarot or oracle decks to see which ones resonate most strongly with you and your learning goals.

Through the practice of this Daily Learning Card Spell, you open yourself to the guidance and wisdom of the cards, allowing them to illuminate your path of learning and growth. May each card drawn bring you closer to your goals and deepen your understanding of yourself and the world around you.

37. GRATITUDE STONE CIRCLE SPELL

Ingredients:
- Several small stones or crystals (preferably smooth and comfortable to sit on)
- A quiet and comfortable outdoor or indoor space

Spell Instructions:
1. Prepare Your Space:
   - Choose a quiet and comfortable space where you can sit undisturbed for the duration of the spell. This can be outdoors in nature or indoors in a peaceful room.

2. Gather Your Stones:
   - Collect several small stones or crystals to create your circle of gratitude. Choose stones that resonate with you and evoke feelings of gratitude and abundance.

3. Create the Circle:
   - Arrange the stones in a circle around you, leaving an opening large enough for you to sit comfortably within the circle. As you place each stone, infuse it with feelings of gratitude and appreciation.

4. Sit Within the Circle:
   - Once the circle is complete, take a moment to center yourself and connect with the energy of the stones surrounding you. Sit comfortably within the circle, feeling supported and embraced by the energy of gratitude.

5. Reflect on Your Growth:
   - Close your eyes and take several deep breaths to ground yourself in the present moment. Reflect on your journey of growth and personal development, acknowledging the progress you've made and the challenges you've overcome.

6. Express Gratitude:
   - With each breath, allow feelings of gratitude to fill your heart and mind. Think about the people, experiences, and opportunities that have contributed to your growth, and express thanks for them.

7. Visualize Abundance:
   - Visualize your circle of gratitude expanding outward, radiating waves of gratitude and abundance into the universe. Imagine these waves rippling outward, touching the lives of others and amplifying the energy of gratitude in the world.

8. Set Intentions:
   - Set intentions for continued growth and abundance in your life. Affirm your commitment to nurturing a mindset of gratitude and embracing each new

experience as an opportunity for growth.

9. Sit in Silence:
 - Spend several minutes sitting in silence within the circle, allowing the energy of gratitude to permeate your being. Be open to any insights or messages that may arise during this time of reflection.

10. Close the Circle:
 - When you feel ready, gently open your eyes and take a moment to thank the stones for their support and the energy they've provided during the spell. Slowly rise from your seated position, knowing that the circle of gratitude remains with you wherever you go.

Additional Tips:
- You can enhance the potency of this spell by incorporating other elements of nature, such as flowers, leaves, or shells, into your gratitude circle.
- Consider incorporating a gratitude meditation or affirmation practice into your daily routine to cultivate an ongoing sense of gratitude and abundance in your life.

Through the practice of this Gratitude Stone Circle Spell, you tap into the transformative power of gratitude, creating a sacred space to reflect on your growth and express thanks for the blessings in your life. May the energy of gratitude continue to guide and support you on your journey of personal and spiritual

THE WELLNESS WITCH

evolution.

38. VISUALIZATION CANDLE SPELL

Ingredients:
- A candle (choose a color that resonates with your goal, such as green for abundance, yellow for success, or white for clarity)
- A quiet and comfortable space

Spell Instructions:
1. Prepare Your Space:
    - Find a quiet and comfortable space where you can perform the visualization spell without interruptions. Create a sacred atmosphere by dimming the lights and setting the mood with soothing music or incense if desired.

2. Set Your Intention:
    - Hold the candle in your hands and set your intention for the spell. Visualize your goal clearly in your mind and affirm your commitment to achieving it.

3. Light the Candle:
    - Place the candle on a flat surface in front of you. Take a moment to admire the flame as it dances and flickers, symbolizing the energy and passion you're

investing in your goal.

4. Focus Your Mind:
 - Close your eyes and take a few deep breaths to center yourself. Clear your mind of any distractions and focus your attention solely on the flame of the candle.

5. Visualize Your Goal:
 - As you gaze at the flame, begin to visualize yourself achieving your goal in vivid detail. Imagine every aspect of the experience, from the sights and sounds to the emotions you'll feel when you succeed.

6. Focus on the Steps:
 - Now, shift your focus to the steps you need to take to reach your goal. Visualize yourself taking each step with confidence and determination, overcoming obstacles along the way.

7. Feel the Success:
 - Allow yourself to immerse fully in the visualization, feeling the excitement and fulfillment of achieving your goal as if it were already a reality. Let this feeling of success wash over you, filling you with confidence and motivation.

8. Express Gratitude:
 - With gratitude in your heart, thank the universe (or any higher power you believe in) for supporting you on your journey toward your goal. Express thanks

for the opportunities and resources that will help you manifest your vision.

9. Seal Your Intentions:
   - Blow out the candle, symbolizing the completion of the visualization spell and the release of your intentions into the universe. Trust that the energy you've infused into the candle will continue to work on your behalf.

10. Take Inspired Action:
    - After performing the visualization spell, take inspired action toward your goal. Remain open to opportunities and follow your intuition as you move forward on your path to success.

Additional Tips:
- You can enhance the potency of this spell by incorporating affirmations or mantras related to your goal into your visualization practice.
- Practice this visualization spell regularly, preferably at the same time each day, to reinforce your intentions and keep your focus sharp.
- Keep a journal to record any insights, inspirations, or synchronicities that arise during your visualization sessions.

Through the practice of this Visualization Candle Spell, you harness the power of focused intention and visualization to manifest your goals and dreams. May the flame of the candle ignite the spark of possibility within you, guiding you toward the realization of your deepest desires.

39. HEART CHAKRA MEDITATION SPELL

Ingredients:
- A quiet and comfortable space
- Optional: soothing music or incense

Spell Instructions:
1. Prepare Your Space:
   - Find a quiet and comfortable space where you can sit or lie down undisturbed for the duration of the meditation. Dim the lights and create a serene atmosphere by lighting candles or burning incense if desired.

2. Get into a Comfortable Position:
   - Sit or lie down in a comfortable position, ensuring that your spine is straight and your body is relaxed. Close your eyes and take a few deep breaths to center yourself.

3. Connect with Your Breath:
   - Begin to focus on your breath, allowing it to become slow, deep, and rhythmic. With each inhale, imagine drawing in love and compassion. With each exhale, release any tension or negativity from your body.

4. Focus on Your Heart Center:
   - Bring your awareness to the center of your chest, where your heart chakra resides. Visualize a radiant green light glowing at this center, representing the energy of love, compassion, and growth.

5. Open Your Heart Chakra:
   - As you continue to breathe deeply, imagine this green light expanding with each breath, gradually filling your chest cavity and surrounding your entire body. Feel your heart chakra opening and expanding, allowing love and growth to flow freely.

6. Visualize Growth and Learning:
   - With your heart chakra fully open, visualize a stream of golden light flowing into it, carrying with it the energy of growth and learning. See this light infusing every cell of your being, nurturing your soul and expanding your consciousness.

7. Affirmations of Growth:
   - Repeat affirmations silently or aloud that affirm your commitment to growth and learning. For example, you could say, "I am open to growth and learning. I embrace every experience as an opportunity for growth."

8. Feel the Energy:
   - Allow yourself to bask in the energy of your open heart chakra and the influx of growth and learning energy. Notice any sensations or emotions that arise

as you connect with this energy.

9. Express Gratitude:
   - Take a moment to express gratitude for the growth and learning opportunities that come your way. Feel thankful for the experiences that have shaped you into the person you are today.

10. Close the Meditation:
    - When you feel ready, slowly bring your awareness back to your physical surroundings. Wiggle your fingers and toes, gently stretch your body, and open your eyes. Take a few moments to reflect on your experience before returning to your day.

Additional Tips:
- You can enhance the potency of this meditation by incorporating heart-opening yoga poses or heart-centered affirmations into your practice.
- Practice this Heart Chakra Meditation regularly, preferably daily, to keep your heart chakra open and receptive to growth and learning opportunities.

Through the practice of this Heart Chakra Meditation Spell, you align yourself with the energy of love and growth, nurturing your soul and expanding your consciousness. May your heart chakra remain open and receptive, allowing you to embrace every experience as an opportunity for growth and learning.

40. POSITIVE AFFIRMATION RITUAL SPELL

Ingredients:
- A quiet and comfortable space
- Your chosen positive affirmation

Spell Instructions:
1. Prepare Your Space:
   - Find a quiet and comfortable space where you can sit or stand undisturbed for the duration of the ritual. Dim the lights and create a serene atmosphere with soothing music or incense if desired.

2. Select Your Affirmation:
   - Choose a positive affirmation that resonates with you and aligns with your intentions for growth and empowerment. It could be a simple phrase like "I am worthy" or "I am capable."

3. Set Your Intention:
   - Hold your chosen affirmation in your mind and set your intention for the ritual. Affirm your commitment to embracing positivity and self-empowerment as you repeat the affirmation.

4. Center Yourself:
 - Take a few deep breaths to center yourself and bring your focus inward. Clear your mind of any distractions and open yourself to receive the energy of the affirmation.

5. Repeat the Affirmation:
 - Begin to repeat your chosen affirmation either silently or aloud, allowing each word to resonate deeply within you. Feel the truth and power of the affirmation as you speak it, affirming it with conviction.

6. Visualize the Affirmation:
 - As you continue to repeat the affirmation, visualize its truth manifesting in your life. Imagine yourself embodying the qualities and characteristics expressed in the affirmation, feeling them becoming more and more real with each repetition.

7. Feel the Positive Energy:
 - Allow yourself to bask in the positive energy of the affirmation, feeling it uplift and empower you from within. Notice any shifts in your mood or mindset as you connect with the affirmation on a deeper level.

8. Express Gratitude:
 - Take a moment to express gratitude for the affirmation and the positive energy it brings into your life. Acknowledge the power of your words and

intentions to shape your reality.

9. Integrate the Affirmation:
   - Carry the energy of the affirmation with you throughout your day, repeating it whenever you need a boost of positivity or encouragement. Let it serve as a guiding light on your path to growth and self-empowerment.

10. Close the Ritual:
    - When you feel ready, slowly release the energy of the ritual and return to your normal state of consciousness. Take a moment to ground yourself before continuing with your day, knowing that the power of your affirmation is with you always.

Additional Tips:
- Write down your chosen affirmation and place it somewhere visible, such as on your mirror or computer screen, to serve as a constant reminder of your intention.
- Practice this Positive Affirmation Ritual daily or as needed to reinforce the positive beliefs and intentions you wish to cultivate in your life.

Through the practice of this Positive Affirmation Ritual Spell, you harness the power of positive words and intentions to uplift and empower yourself. May your chosen affirmation serve as a beacon of light, guiding you toward a life filled with joy, abundance, and self-empowerment.

41. LEARNING TREE SPELL

Ingredients:
- Paper or canvas
- Drawing or painting materials
- Pen or marker

Spell Instructions:
1. Prepare Your Materials:
   - Gather your paper or canvas along with your drawing or painting materials. Find a comfortable and quiet space where you can focus on your creation.

2. Set Your Intention:
   - Hold your pen or marker in your hand and set your intention for the spell. Visualize yourself embarking on a journey of continuous learning and growth as you begin to create your Learning Tree.

3. Draw or Paint Your Tree:
   - Using your chosen medium, draw or paint the outline of a tree on the paper or canvas. Let your creativity flow as you design the branches, trunk, and roots of your tree. Feel a connection to the natural world as you bring your tree to life.

4. Add Your Leaves:

- As you continue to work on your tree, add a leaf to each branch for every new thing you learn. Write or draw something that represents what you've learned on each leaf. Allow the tree to grow and flourish with each new addition.

5. Reflect on Your Growth:
 - Take a moment to reflect on your Learning Tree as it begins to fill with leaves. Notice how it represents your journey of growth and discovery, with each leaf symbolizing a new experience or piece of knowledge gained.

6. Express Gratitude:
 - Express gratitude for the opportunities to learn and grow that come your way. Appreciate the abundance of knowledge and wisdom available to you as you continue to nurture your Learning Tree.

7. Place Your Tree:
 - Once your Learning Tree is complete, find a special place to display it where you can see it regularly. Let it serve as a visual reminder of your commitment to lifelong learning and personal growth.

8. Visit Your Tree:
 - Regularly visit your Learning Tree to add new leaves and reflect on your progress. Take pride in watching it grow and evolve over time, knowing that each leaf represents a step forward on your journey.

Additional Tips:
- You can personalize your Learning Tree by adding colors, decorations, or additional elements that resonate with you and your learning journey.
- Consider sharing your Learning Tree with others as a source of inspiration and encouragement for their own paths of growth and discovery.

Through the practice of this Learning Tree Spell, you create a tangible representation of your commitment to lifelong learning and personal growth. May your Learning Tree flourish and thrive, serving as a constant reminder of the beauty and richness of the journey ahead.

42. CLEANSING RITUAL SPELL

Ingredients:
- Sage bundle or Palo Santo stick
- Fireproof dish or container

Spell Instructions:
1. Prepare Your Space:
   - Begin by finding a quiet and clutter-free area where you can perform the cleansing ritual without interruption. Open windows or doors to allow fresh air to flow through the space.

2. Set Your Intention:
   - Hold the sage bundle or Palo Santo stick in your hands and take a few deep breaths to center yourself. Close your eyes and visualize the space being filled with bright, cleansing energy.

3. Light the Sage or Palo Santo:
   - Using a lighter or match, carefully ignite the tip of the sage bundle or Palo Santo stick until it begins to smolder and release smoke. Allow the flame to extinguish naturally, leaving behind a steady stream of smoke.

4. Begin Cleansing:
   - Starting at the entrance of the space, walk clockwise around the room, moving the sage bundle or Palo Santo stick in a sweeping motion. Focus on areas where energy may feel stagnant or heavy, such as corners and doorways.

5. Set Your Intention:
   - As you move through the space, set the intention to release any negative or limiting beliefs that may be lingering. Visualize these beliefs being swept away by the smoke, leaving behind a clear and open space for growth.

6. Affirm Your Growth Mindset:
   - While performing the cleansing ritual, affirm your commitment to embracing a growth mindset. Repeat positive affirmations such as "I am open to new possibilities" or "I embrace challenges as opportunities for growth."

7. Express Gratitude:
   - As you complete the cleansing ritual, express gratitude for the opportunity to release old energy and welcome in fresh, positive vibrations. Thank the sage or Palo Santo for its cleansing properties.

8. Extinguish the Sage or Palo Santo:
   - Once you have finished cleansing the space, gently extinguish the sage bundle or Palo Santo stick by pressing it into the fireproof dish or container until

the smoke dissipates.

9. Close the Ritual:
 - Take a moment to center yourself and reflect on the renewed energy of the space. Offer a final affirmation of your commitment to growth and transformation before concluding the ritual.

Additional Tips:
- You can enhance the potency of the cleansing ritual by incorporating other tools such as crystals, sound bowls, or essential oils that resonate with your intention for growth.
- Repeat this cleansing ritual regularly, especially during times of transition or when you feel the need to refresh the energy of your space.

Through the practice of this Cleansing Ritual Spell, you create a harmonious environment that supports your journey towards a growth mindset. May the smoke of the sage or Palo Santo cleanse away any obstacles to growth, leaving behind a space filled with clarity, positivity, and possibility.

43. GRATITUDE JOURNAL SPELL

Ingredients:
- Blank journal or notebook
- Pen or pencil

Spell Instructions:
1. Prepare Your Journal:
   - Begin by selecting a blank journal or notebook that resonates with you. Choose one with pages that feel inviting and conducive to writing.

2. Set Your Intention:
   - Hold the journal in your hands and take a few deep breaths to center yourself. Set your intention for the journal, focusing on gratitude and growth.

3. Dedicate Your Journal:
   - Write a dedication on the first page of the journal, expressing your commitment to using it as a tool for gratitude and reflection on your learning journey.

4. Daily Entries:
   - Each day, take a few moments to sit with your journal and reflect on your experiences and growth. Write down at least one thing you're grateful for

related to your learning journey.

5. Express Your Appreciation:
 - As you write, allow yourself to fully experience the gratitude you feel for the opportunities for growth and learning in your life. Reflect on how each experience contributes to your personal development.

6. Reflect on Your Growth:
 - Take time to reflect on your progress and accomplishments, no matter how small they may seem. Celebrate your successes and acknowledge the steps you've taken towards your goals.

7. Affirm Your Intentions:
 - Before closing each journal entry, affirm your intentions for continued growth and gratitude. Repeat positive affirmations such as "I am grateful for the opportunities to learn and grow" or "I embrace each day with an open heart and mind."

8. Regular Practice:
 - Make writing in your gratitude journal a regular practice, whether it's daily, weekly, or whenever you feel called to reflect on your experiences. Consistency is key to deepening your gratitude practice.

Additional Tips:
- Enhance your gratitude journaling practice by incorporating other creative elements such as

drawing, painting, or collage to visually represent your reflections and experiences.
- Keep your gratitude journal in a place where you'll see it often, such as on your bedside table or desk, to serve as a reminder to pause and express gratitude regularly.

Through the practice of this Gratitude Journal Spell, you cultivate a deeper sense of appreciation for your learning journey and the growth opportunities it presents. May your journal be a source of inspiration and reflection, guiding you towards greater self-awareness, gratitude, and fulfillment.

44. FLOWER CROWN RITUAL SPELL

Ingredients:
- Fresh flowers (such as sunflowers, daisies, or any flowers symbolizing growth)
- Floral wire or flexible green wire
- Wire cutters or scissors

Spell Instructions:
1. Gather Your Materials:
    - Begin by gathering your fresh flowers and floral wire. Choose flowers that symbolize growth, abundance, and vitality, such as sunflowers, daisies, or any other blooms that resonate with you.

2. Set Your Intention:
    - Find a quiet and peaceful space where you can focus on crafting your flower crown. Take a few moments to center yourself and set your intention for the ritual. Visualize the crown as a symbol of your own growth and potential.

3. Prepare Your Flowers:
    - Carefully trim the stems of your flowers to a manageable length, leaving enough to secure them to the crown. Remove any excess leaves or thorns that

may obstruct the wire.

4. Create the Crown Base:
   - Take the floral wire and measure it around your head, leaving a little extra length for adjustments. Shape the wire into a circle and secure the ends by twisting them together.

5. Attach the Flowers:
   - Begin attaching the flowers to the crown base by weaving their stems through the wire. Arrange them in a pleasing pattern, alternating colors and sizes to create visual interest. Secure each flower in place by twisting the wire around its stem.

6. Set Your Intention:
   - As you work on the flower crown, focus on your intention for growth and transformation. Visualize each flower as a symbol of your own personal journey, blossoming and flourishing with each new experience.

7. Infuse with Energy:
   - Once the flower crown is complete, hold it in your hands and infuse it with your energy and intentions. Imagine the crown radiating with vibrant energy, imbued with the essence of growth and vitality.

8. Wear Your Crown:
   - Place the flower crown upon your head, allowing its petals to brush against your skin. Feel the energy of

the flowers enveloping you, filling you with a sense of renewal and empowerment.

9. Meditation or Ritual:
   - Sit quietly with your flower crown, either in meditation or during a ritual practice. Allow yourself to connect with the energy of the crown and the symbolism of growth it represents. Visualize yourself embracing new opportunities and blossoming into your fullest potential.

Additional Tips:
- Consider incorporating other elements into your flower crown, such as crystals, feathers, or ribbons, to enhance its magical properties and personalize it to your intentions.
- After wearing your flower crown, you can preserve it by carefully removing the flowers and pressing them between the pages of a heavy book or using them in other magical rituals.

Through the practice of this Flower Crown Ritual Spell, you honor your journey of growth and transformation, embracing the beauty and vitality of the natural world as you step into your own power and potential. May your flower crown serve as a reminder of the limitless possibilities that await you on your path of growth and expansion.

45. SELF-LOVE MEDITATION SPELL

Spell Instructions:
1. Prepare Your Space:
   - Find a quiet and comfortable space where you can sit or lie down without distractions. Dim the lights, if possible, and create a serene atmosphere.

2. Center Yourself:
   - Take a few deep breaths to center yourself and release any tension or stress from your body. Close your eyes and allow yourself to relax into the present moment.

3. Set Your Intention:
   - Set your intention for the meditation, focusing on cultivating self-love and embracing your potential for growth and transformation. Visualize yourself surrounded by a warm, loving energy.

4. Connect with Your Heart Center:
   - Place one hand over your heart center, just above your chest, and take a few moments to connect with the energy of your heart. Feel its gentle rhythm and the warmth emanating from within.

5. Visualize a Pink or Green Light:
   - Visualize a soft pink or green light glowing at your heart center, symbolizing love, compassion, and growth. As you breathe deeply, imagine this light expanding with each inhale, filling your entire being with love and acceptance.

6. Affirmations of Self-Love:
   - Repeat affirmations of self-love silently or aloud, such as "I am worthy of love and acceptance," "I embrace my strengths and weaknesses," or "I am deserving of happiness and fulfillment."

7. Embrace Your Potential:
   - Visualize yourself as a seedling, planted firmly in the rich soil of self-love. Envision your roots growing deeper and stronger, anchoring you in your worth and potential. See yourself growing taller and reaching towards the light, blossoming into your fullest expression.

8. Release Self-Doubt:
   - Release any self-doubt or limiting beliefs that may be holding you back from fully embracing your self-love and potential. Let go of negative thoughts or judgments, allowing them to dissolve into the loving energy surrounding you.

9. Gratitude for Self-Love:
   - Express gratitude for the love and acceptance you have for yourself. Acknowledge the progress you've

made on your journey of self-love and growth, and celebrate the love that exists within you.

10. Closing the Meditation:
   - Take a few more deep breaths, feeling the energy of self-love and empowerment radiating throughout your entire being. When you feel ready, slowly open your eyes and return to the present moment, carrying the warmth of self-love with you.

Additional Tips:
- You can enhance your self-love meditation by incorporating gentle movements or stretches to release tension from your body and further connect with your heart center.
- Practice this meditation regularly, ideally daily, to deepen your connection with self-love and cultivate a greater sense of empowerment and potential.

Through the practice of this Self-Love Meditation Spell, you nurture a deep and unconditional love for yourself, recognizing your inherent worthiness and embracing your limitless potential for growth and transformation. May the energy of self-love guide you on your journey towards wholeness and fulfillment.

46. POSITIVE LETTER FROM THE UNIVERSE SPELL

Spell Instructions:
1. Prepare Your Writing Space:
 - Find a quiet and comfortable space where you can focus on connecting with the energy of the universe. Light a candle or burn some incense to create a sacred atmosphere.

2. Center Yourself:
 - Take a few deep breaths to center yourself and clear your mind of any distractions. Close your eyes and envision yourself surrounded by a warm, loving light.

3. Set Your Intention:
 - Set your intention for the spell, focusing on receiving a positive message of encouragement and belief in your growth potential from the universe.

4. Begin Writing:
 - Take a piece of paper or open a blank document on your computer. Start writing the letter as if it were from the universe itself. Address it to yourself, using phrases like "Dear [Your Name]" or "Beloved Soul."

5. Express Unconditional Love:

- In the letter, express unconditional love and acceptance for yourself. Remind yourself of your inherent worthiness and the limitless potential that resides within you.

6. Acknowledge Your Growth:
   - Acknowledge the growth you've experienced on your journey and celebrate your accomplishments, no matter how small they may seem. Reflect on the progress you've made and the challenges you've overcome.

7. Encourage Further Expansion:
   - Encourage yourself to continue expanding and evolving, trusting in your ability to navigate life's twists and turns with grace and resilience. Affirm your belief in your own growth potential.

8. Offer Words of Wisdom:
   - Offer words of wisdom and guidance from the perspective of the universe. Share insights or intuitive messages that resonate with your soul and inspire you to keep moving forward.

9. Seal the Letter:
   - Once you've finished writing the letter, read it aloud to yourself, allowing the words to sink in and resonate deeply within your being. When you feel ready, fold the letter and seal it with a kiss or a drop of candle wax.

SPELLS FOR POSITIVE THINKING AND MENTAL RESILIENCE

10. Keep the Letter Close:
   - Keep the letter in a safe and sacred place where you can revisit it whenever you need a reminder of the universe's unwavering belief in your growth potential.

Additional Tips:
- You can enhance the power of this spell by performing it during a full moon or other auspicious cosmic event when the energy of the universe is heightened.
- Consider decorating the letter with symbols or images that hold personal significance for you, further imbuing it with positive energy and intention.

Through the practice of this Positive Letter from the Universe Spell, you receive a powerful message of encouragement and belief in your growth potential from the loving embrace of the cosmos. May the wisdom and love contained within the letter guide you on your journey towards greater expansion and fulfillment.

47. AFFIRMATION ART SPELL

Spell Instructions:
1. Gather Your Art Supplies:
   - Collect your art supplies, including canvas or paper, paints, markers, colored pencils, or any other materials you prefer for creating your artwork.

2. Set Your Intention:
   - Sit in a quiet and comfortable space where you can focus on your creative process. Take a few deep breaths to center yourself and set your intention for the spell.

3. Choose Your Affirmations:
   - Select affirmations that resonate with your desire for growth and empowerment. These can be phrases like "I am constantly evolving," "I embrace change with courage," or "I am open to new opportunities for growth."

4. Create Your Artwork:
   - Begin to create your piece of art, allowing your intuition to guide you as you incorporate your chosen affirmations into the design. Use colors, shapes, and symbols that evoke feelings of growth, expansion,

and positivity.

5. Infuse with Intention:
 - As you work on your artwork, infuse it with your intention for growth and empowerment. Visualize your affirmations coming to life on the canvas, radiating with vibrant energy and power.

6. Focus on the Process:
 - Stay present in the moment as you create, allowing the act of art-making to become a form of meditation. Let go of any self-judgment or perfectionism, and instead, focus on the joy and expression of the creative process.

7. Charge Your Artwork:
 - Once your artwork is complete, hold it in your hands and charge it with your intention for growth and empowerment. Visualize your affirmations activating within the artwork, infusing it with positive energy.

8. Hang Your Artwork:
 - Find a prominent place in your home where you can hang your artwork where you'll see it daily. Choose a location where it can serve as a constant reminder of your commitment to growth and empowerment.

9. Activate Daily Affirmations:
 - Each time you see your artwork, take a moment to pause and recite the affirmations aloud or silently to

yourself. Allow the energy of the artwork to uplift and inspire you on your journey of growth.

Additional Tips:
- You can enhance the power of your affirmation art by incorporating additional magical elements such as crystals, herbs, or symbols that hold personal significance for you.
- Consider creating multiple pieces of affirmation art to place in different areas of your home, spreading the energy of growth and empowerment throughout your space.

Through the practice of this Affirmation Art Spell, you harness the power of creativity and intention to manifest your desires for growth and empowerment. May your artwork serve as a powerful tool for transformation, inspiring you to embrace your journey with courage and confidence.

48. DAILY GROWTH CARD SPELL

Spell Instructions:
1. Prepare Your Card Deck:
 - Gather a deck of cards, such as oracle cards or affirmation cards, that contain growth-related affirmations, quotes, or messages. If you don't have a specific deck, you can create your own by writing affirmations on index cards or pieces of paper.

2. Set Your Intention:
 - Sit in a quiet and comfortable space where you can focus on connecting with the energy of growth and expansion. Take a few deep breaths to center yourself and set your intention for the spell.

3. Shuffle the Cards:
 - Hold the deck of cards in your hands and shuffle them while focusing on your intention for growth and personal development. As you shuffle, visualize the cards being infused with positive energy and guidance.

4. Draw a Card:
 - When you feel ready, draw a single card from the deck. Trust that the card you draw holds a message

that is meant for you and your journey of growth.

5. Reflect on the Message:
   - Take a moment to study the card you've drawn. Read the affirmation or quote aloud, allowing the words to sink in and resonate with you. Reflect on how the message applies to your current circumstances and what insights it offers for your path of growth.

6. Embrace the Guidance:
   - Embrace the guidance offered by the card and allow its wisdom to inspire you throughout the day. Consider how you can apply the message in practical ways to support your personal development and expansion.

7. Carry the Message with You:
   - Keep the card with you throughout the day as a reminder of the growth-oriented energy you've invoked. Place it in your pocket, wallet, or somewhere else where you'll see it frequently.

8. Act on the Insight:
   - Throughout the day, reflect on the message of the card and look for opportunities to embody its wisdom in your thoughts, words, and actions. Use it as a source of inspiration and motivation to take positive steps towards your goals.

Additional Tips:

- You can enhance the power of this spell by performing it during a time when you feel particularly open to receiving guidance and insights, such as during a meditation or quiet contemplation session.
- Consider keeping a journal where you can record the messages you receive from your daily growth cards and reflect on how they impact your journey of personal development.

Through the practice of this Daily Growth Card Spell, you open yourself up to the guidance and wisdom of the universe, allowing it to support you on your path of growth and expansion. May each card you draw serve as a beacon of inspiration and empowerment, guiding you towards greater levels of fulfillment and success.

49. SUNRISE AFFIRMATIONS SPELL

Spell Instructions:
1. Prepare for Sunrise:
 - Wake up early enough to witness the sunrise. Find a quiet and comfortable spot where you can observe the sun as it begins to peek over the horizon. Dress warmly if necessary and bring a blanket or cushion to sit on.

2. Set Your Intention:
 - Stand or sit in a comfortable position, facing the direction where the sun will rise. Close your eyes and take several deep breaths to center yourself. Set your intention for the spell, focusing on welcoming the new day's opportunities for growth and transformation.

3. Connect with Nature:
 - As you wait for the sun to rise, take a moment to connect with the natural world around you. Listen to the sounds of birds singing, feel the cool morning breeze on your skin, and appreciate the beauty of the world awakening around you.

4. Recite Affirmations:

- As the first light of dawn appears on the horizon, begin reciting growth affirmations aloud or silently to yourself. Choose affirmations that resonate with your desire for personal development, expansion, and empowerment. Some examples include:
    - "With each sunrise, I welcome new opportunities for growth and transformation."
    - "I embrace change as a natural part of my journey towards self-improvement."
    - "Today, I choose to step out of my comfort zone and explore new possibilities for growth."
    - "I am open to receiving the lessons and blessings that each new day brings."

5. Visualize Your Goals:
    - As you recite your affirmations, visualize yourself embracing the opportunities for growth that the new day presents. Imagine yourself stepping confidently into the future, ready to overcome challenges and achieve your goals.

6. Express Gratitude:
    - Before the sun fully rises, take a moment to express gratitude for the blessings in your life and the opportunities for growth that lie ahead. Offer thanks to the universe for the gift of another day and the chance to continue your journey of self-discovery.

7. Witness the Sunrise:
    - As the sun rises above the horizon, take a moment to bask in its warm glow and absorb its energy. Feel a

sense of renewal and vitality washing over you as you welcome the dawn of a new day filled with endless possibilities.

8. Close the Spell:
 - When you feel ready, gently open your eyes and take one final deep breath. Offer a silent prayer of gratitude to the sun for its life-giving energy and the inspiration it provides. Carry the energy of the sunrise with you throughout the day as a reminder of your commitment to growth and transformation.

Additional Tips:
- You can enhance the power of this spell by performing it outdoors in a natural setting, such as a park, beach, or mountaintop, where you have a clear view of the sunrise.
- Consider keeping a journal where you can write down any insights or inspirations that arise during your sunrise affirmations practice, allowing you to track your progress and reflect on your growth over time.

Through the practice of this Sunrise Affirmations Spell, you harness the transformative energy of the sunrise to set powerful intentions for growth and empowerment at the start of each new day. May the light of the rising sun illuminate your path and guide you towards greater levels of fulfillment and success in all areas of your life.

50. GRATITUDE CANDLE SPELL

Spell Instructions:

1. Prepare Your Candle:
   - Choose a candle that resonates with you for this spell. It could be a color that represents gratitude to you, such as yellow or gold, or any candle that you feel drawn to for expressing gratitude.

2. Set Your Sacred Space:
   - Find a quiet and comfortable space where you can perform the spell without interruption. Clear the area of any clutter and set up your candle on a safe and stable surface, such as an altar or tabletop.

3. Center Yourself:
   - Take a few moments to center yourself and ground your energy. Close your eyes and take several deep breaths, allowing yourself to relax and enter a state of calm and receptivity.

4. Light the Candle:
   - Using a match or lighter, gently ignite the candle flame. As you do so, visualize the flame as a beacon of gratitude, radiating warmth and light throughout your space.

5. Express Gratitude:
   - With the candle flame as your focal point, begin to express gratitude for the growth experiences you've had throughout the day. Speak from the heart and allow your words to flow freely as you reflect on the blessings and lessons you've received.

6. Be Specific:
   - Try to be as specific as possible in your expressions of gratitude. Acknowledge the challenges you've faced and the ways in which you've grown from them. Recognize the support and guidance you've received from others, as well as the moments of insight and inspiration that have come your way.

7. Visualize Growth:
   - As you express gratitude, visualize the energy of your gratitude expanding outward from the candle flame, filling your space with warmth and positivity. See yourself surrounded by a golden glow of appreciation, embracing the growth experiences of the day with an open heart.

8. Seal Your Intentions:
   - Once you've expressed your gratitude fully, take a moment to seal your intentions for continued growth and abundance. Visualize the flame of the candle as a symbol of your intentions being sent out into the universe, where they will manifest and multiply in the days to come.

9. Close the Spell:
- When you feel ready, gently blow out the candle flame, if safe to do so, or extinguish it with a candle snuffer. As you do, offer a final word of thanks for the opportunity to express gratitude and set intentions for growth. Carry the energy of gratitude with you as you move forward into the night.

Additional Tips:
- You can enhance the power of this spell by incorporating other elements that resonate with you, such as crystals, incense, or essential oils that evoke feelings of gratitude and abundance.
- Consider keeping a gratitude journal where you can write down your daily expressions of gratitude, allowing you to track your progress and cultivate a deeper sense of appreciation for the growth experiences in your life.

Through the practice of this Gratitude Candle Spell, you create a sacred space for expressing gratitude and setting intentions for continued growth and abundance. May the light of the candle illuminate your path and guide you towards greater levels of fulfillment and success in all areas of your life.

Printed in Great Britain
by Amazon